SAGA OF THE SWAMP THING BOOK TWO

Written by Alan Moore Len Wein

Art by Stephen Bissette John Totleben Shawn McManus
Rick Veitch Alfredo Alcala Ron Randall Berni Wrightson

Colored by Tatjana Wood

Lettered by John Costanza

Original Series Cover Art by Stephen Bissette John Totleben

Original Series Cover Color by Tatjana Wood

Swamp Thing created by Len Wein and Bernie Wrightson

SAGA OF THE SWAMP THING

BOOK TWO

Karen Berger Editor – Original Series
Scott Nybakken Editor
Robbin Brosterman Design Director – Books
Louis Prandi Publication Design

Karen Berger Senior VP – Executive Editor, Vertigo
Bob Harras VP – Editor-in-Chief

Diane Nelson President
Dan DiDio and **Jim Lee** Co-Publishers
Geoff Johns Chief Creative Officer
John Rood Executive VP – Sales, Marketing and Business Development
Amy Genkins Senior VP – Business and Legal Affairs
Nairi Gardiner Senior VP – Finance
Jeff Boison VP – Publishing Operations
Mark Chiarello VP – Art Direction and Design
John Cunningham VP – Marketing
Terri Cunningham VP – Talent Relations and Services
Alison Gill Senior VP – Manufacturing and Operations
Hank Kanalz Senior VP – Digital
Jay Kogan VP – Business and Legal Affairs, Publishing
Jack Mahan VP – Business Affairs, Talent
Nick Napolitano VP – Manufacturing Administration
Sue Pohja VP – Book Sales
Courtney Simmons Senior VP – Publicity
Bob Wayne Senior VP – Sales

Cover pencils by **Stephen Bissette.**
Cover inks by **John Totleben.**
Cover color by **Allen Passalaqua.**
Color reconstruction on selected interior pages by **Drew Moore.**

SAGA OF THE SWAMP THING BOOK TWO
Published by DC Comics.

DC Comics
1700 Broadway,
New York, NY 10019
A Warner Bros. Entertainment Company.
Printed in the USA.
First Printing.
ISBN: 978-1-4012-2544-5

Library of Congress Cataloging-in-Publication Data

Moore, Alan, 1953-
Saga of the Swamp Thing book two / Alan Moore, Stephen Bissette, John Totleben.
p. cm.
"Originally published as The Saga Of The Swamp Thing 28-34 And Swamp Thing Annual 2."
ISBN 978-1-4012-2544-5 (alk. paper)
1. Graphic novels. I. Bissette, Stephen. II. Totleben, John. III. Title.
PN6728.S93M653 2012
741.5'973—dc23
2012023064

SUSTAINABLE FORESTRY INITIATIVE
Certified Chain of Custody
Promoting Sustainable Forestry
www.sfiprogram.org
SFI-01042
APPLIES TO TEXT STOCK ONLY

Introduction

It seems like a long time ago — swollen torrents of words have roared under many bridges; oceans of exotic imagery have swirled and risen; the shapes of continents have changed. Strange, how one's life passes. When I first read these stories, I was an aspiring comics writer who had barely begun to appreciate the skill and potential of the careful alchemical wedding of words and pictures which Alan Moore was daily practicing with love and dedication. Following a small but worthy tradition of adepts, Moore was working to transform the medium of his choice from what I, in common with many others, had regarded as an often cynically produced, pile-it-high, sell-it-cheap form of entertainment into something vital — something with currency.

I was always a slow learner. You can lead a horse to water but you can't make him drink — unless you hold his head under.

Rereading these stories for the first time, I am reminded how complacently adaptable humanity is as a species. Most change, we quickly learn to take for granted — short memories, a dangerous lack of vision, a lack of dangerous vision.

Some stories make a difference.

An adolescent poet once described Moore — with a touch of envy, perhaps — as having... purple orchids in his mind. Well, the heat and humidity of the Louisiana swamplands certainly brought them into full, gorgeous bloom and propagated them through the fertile imaginations and inkwells of Steve Bissette and John Totleben and others — to the lasting enrichment of all our lives.

I mentioned love (did I hear a rumor it was fashionable again?). Moore's and his collaborators' obvious love for and faith in their work is what seems to me to glow through these pages — most brightly vegetable, with the charming pathos of the respectful with "Pog" and the celebratory passion of "Rite of Spring," perhaps.

Arriving at "Rite of Spring" (the final story in this volume) seduced by the seeming ease of storytelling and command of the exigencies of serial plotting, we have sympathetically endured and enjoyed the horrors of the characters' lives as Moore gracefully allies us to their personal dramas. We have run the emotional gamut of demons, both terrifyingly crass and devilishly sophisticated, allowing our preconceptions to be disordered so that the mundane becomes exotic and the exotic mundane. Bewildered by the elegant rhythms of the prose and distracted by the ghastly delights of the illustration, we are left softened and raw, uncertain in a world both grotesque and deeply human — grotesquely human. We have been to Hell and

The Comics Code Authority was founded in 1954 by a number of publishers as a self-regulating body, following the outcry against comics (especially the E.C. line of horror comics) set in motion by the comic book witch-hunts of Dr. Frederic Wertham. The code forbade such elements as nudity, rotting zombies, incest and necrophilia, and the combination of these in "Love and Death" was far too rich for the people who administer the Code to handle. It is to DC's credit that, from this point on, rather than trying to tone down the title they chose to put it out without the Code's seal instead.

It was here that the artistic team really began to let loose. Bissette and Totleben give us insects that crawl between panel borders; Abigail Cable dragged into madness and beyond by her late uncle, crouched bloodied and beautiful in a corner; and a Swamp Thing who truly seems like part of the landscape.

(Inquisitive readers might like to know that Messrs. Moore, Bissette and Totleben can be seen in the library copy of *Deadlier Than the Male*, disposing of Young Tammy's remains.)

In "A Halo of Flies," Alfredo Alcala inked Steve Bissette's pencils. Alcala's artwork, if less detailed than Totleben's, is still moody, and reminiscent of old engravings. (An inker, incidentally, goes over a pencil artist's pencils in black ink, finishing the art and making reproduction easier — a good inker adds a great deal to the look, feel, and finish of the strip.)

"The Brimstone Ballet" effectively finishes the Arcane trilogy. Even though the overarching resolution does not occur until the following chapter, these three stories are obviously of a piece, sharing a mood, a bleakly unsettling, sometimes understated perspective of evil, of an approaching Armageddon, and how it affects a woman and her love. Rick Veitch pencilled this episode, allowing Steve Bissette to get a head start on the extra-length story that follows.

That story — "Down Amongst the Dead Men" from *Swamp Thing Annual* #2 — is a change of pace, and one of Moore's most popular Swamp Thing tales, something Moore himself feels has less to do with the story than the subject: What happens after we die?

His answer is classical, harking back to Dante's *The Divine Comedy*. He gives us an immediate afterlife zone of stunned, just-dead spirits and grazing poltergeists, as well as a Paradise — a small, beautiful, balmy place filled with the people one knew and loved. But, just as the most-read and remembered volume of *The Divine Comedy* is *The Inferno*, here the highest point is also the lowest: Hell. A Hades of gross demons, a place of tedium and pain.

While Dante Alighieri had Virgil and Beatrice as his guides, Swamp Thing's guided tour came from four displaced spirits — all of them long-established DC characters.

Deadman was once a circus aerialist named Boston Brand; murdered on the trapeze, he was granted the power to walk the earth whilst hunting his killer — a second chance given by an Oriental goddess named Rama Kushna, portrayed by artist Neal Adams as all eyes, lips, and Zipatone.

The man in the hat and cape is the Phantom Stranger, one of the most ambiguous of DC's characters. Who he is, where he comes from, and what his name is (if he has one) we have never been told. He's generally represented as some kind of agent of Cosmic Balance, appearing when necessary, then walking back into the shadows. Moore hints here at a history and nature for the Stranger that would seem to have begun well before the Fall.

The Spectre came to life — or death — in *More Fun Comics* fifty years ago, when policeman Jim Corrigan was murdered by gangsters. A mysterious light brought Corrigan back from the grave to fight crime as the Spectre. Over the years many different writers have handled the character, with varying takes on his powers, his size, his temper, and his relationship to Jim Corrigan. Here he is seen as some kind of guardian of the borders between Heaven and Hell.

Swamp Thing's final guide is the Demon, created by the man behind so much of what has been exciting in American comics: Jack Kirby, who drew inspiration for the look of the character from the battle mask worn by Hal Foster's *Prince Valiant*. We saw the Demon and his alter ego, Jason Blood (he of the candy-striped hair and the flared eyebrows), in the first *Swamp Thing* collection. Here we see him for the first time in his natural habitat.

These are horror stories: we watch the dead come back and discover the truth of the Black River and recorporations. We learn how to dance the Brimstone Ballet, and what the scariest thing in Arkham Asylum is on the scariest night in its history; and we find out who built Hell — and who builds it to this day.

So by this point, you'd think you would have a good idea of what to expect from *Swamp Thing*: dark messiahs, menaces to humanity, demons, nightmares.

And you'd be right. And you'd be wrong. Where the last three stories in this volume are concerned, at least, you'd be dead wrong.

As I mentioned earlier, sometimes fill-in artists have to step in, and with the amount of time that Bissette and Totleben needed to draw both "Down Amongst the Dead Men" in *Swamp Thing Annual* #2 and "Rite of Spring" in *The Saga of the Swamp Thing* #34, the stories in issues 32 and 33 both had to be fill-ins — but they are none the worse for it.

The first, "Pog," from *The Saga of the Swamp Thing* #32, is my personal favorite of all Alan Moore's Swamp Thing stories. It's a tribute to the work of cartoonist Walt Kelly and his creation, Pogo Possum.

Kelly began his career working for the Walt Disney Studios in the 1930s, and during World War Two he worked as a civilian employee for the army, producing artwork for language manuals. From 1948 to 1949 he was the art director for the short-lived but idealistic newspaper *The New York Star*, for whom he revived a character he had created earlier — Pogo — in the form of a daily comic strip by the same name. When the *Star* folded, *Pogo* went into syndication and was highly successful, lasting until Kelly's death in 1973.

Pogo Possum was part of an ensemble cast made up of inhabitants of the Okefenokee Swamp, scene of many a strange tale and pointed political satire. At a time when almost all other American newspaper strip creators were broadly conservative, Kelly was an unusual animal: a liberal, left-wing cartoonist who used his strip to discuss and parody such targets as the John Birch Society and the McCarthy hearings.

For some time, Moore had wanted to do a tribute in which the swamp-dwelling Pogo met the Swamp Thing. His chance came when he heard that Shawn McManus would be drawing one of the two upcoming fill-in issues. Moore knew that McManus's lighter style would be ideal for the book, as indeed it was.

One of the many delights of "Pog" is Moore's inventive use of language — what Lewis Carroll's Humpty Dumpty referred to as "portmanteau words": neologisms like "millenderings," containing in itself both "millennia" and "wanderings," or "guardiner," with overtones of both gardening and guardianship. This hodge-podge language is a joy to read, a tribute to the dialectical punmanship of Kelly's strip while still being uniquely Moore's. (As an aside, Alan maintains that once he had finished this issue, he found it difficult to write in normal English once more.)

Besides the use of guest artists, another option available to publishers when things are running late is to reprint previously published stories. *The Saga of the Swamp Thing* #33 was originally planned to be an all-reprint issue, but Moore successfully lobbied to add a framing sequence of new material around a single reprinted story. The final product, "Abandoned Houses," was written in a single day, and artist Ron Randall turned in a creditable art job on the shortest of notice.

"Abandoned Houses" is also a tribute, though full comprehension of all of its elements may require some rather esoteric background information.

It has long been a tradition in comics (one that goes back at least as far as E.C.'s

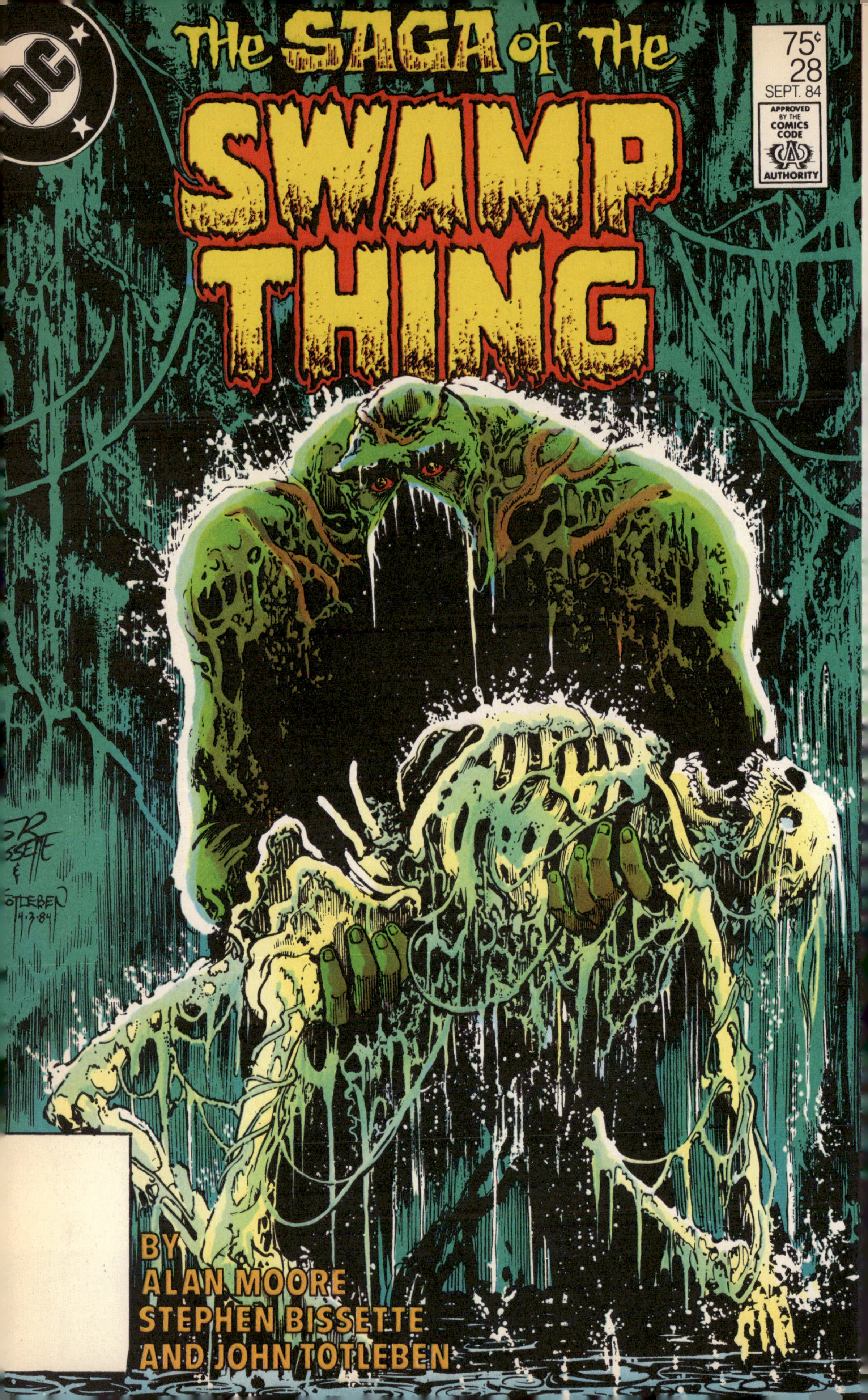
The SAGA of the
SWAMP THING
75¢
28
SEPT. 84
APPROVED BY THE COMICS CODE AUTHORITY
BY
ALAN MOORE
STEPHEN BISSETTE
AND JOHN TOTLEBEN

famous horror titles in the early 1950s) to give horror anthology titles a host as a unifying theme. The host's function was to introduce the short stories and occasionally to come into the last panel and make an appalling pun about the twist ending, of the "Well, readers, Pierre the Hangman proved a real PAIN in the NECK!!" variety. DC's two main horror titles, *The House of Secrets* and *The House of Mystery*, were no exception. Their respective hosts were a fat, slightly terrified demon named Abel and his thinner, worse-tempered brother Cain.

It was in *The House of Secrets*, in 1971, that the very first Swamp Thing story appeared — an eight-page piece that served as a try-out for the original Wein/Wrightson series (and incidentally won the comics equivalent of an Oscar for Best Short Story). By the time that Alan Moore was writing *Swamp Thing*, both *The House of Secrets* and *The House of Mystery* had been cancelled, and on one level "Abandoned Houses" is a tribute to them and to their respective hosts.

Moore had, in 1984, been wondering how to tie that original Swamp Thing tale into the canon, and with this story he got his opportunity. Here he began to explore much of what later became important for the Swamp Thing. Here is the first real sense we get of his role and lineage as an Earth Elemental. Here, too, is the first mention of the Trouble — the long and tortuous learning process that the character would go through in a later episode entitled "American Gothic."

Moore also managed ambiguously to tie Cain and Abel into their Biblical namesakes. (Are they the original Cain and Abel? Or are they, as they variously claim, dreams or right-brain constructs?) This reveals in the process a darker side to the two horror hosts while still allowing them to keep their fair share of secrets and mysteries.

"Rite of Spring," the "vegetable sex" chapter that closes this volume, was responsible for attracting more readers to *Swamp Thing* than ever before. Moore wrote what is essentially a prose poem: an hallucinogenic consummation between a seven-foot-high mound of vegetation and an expatriate Balkan. Many consider this the high point of the series, and the artwork by Bissette and Totleben is outstanding — their personal favorite from their run.

Taken all together, the tales presented in this volume range across the entire emotional spectrum, from the sheer screaming terror of the opening chapters to the strange and wonderful variety of the final third of the book, with its heartwarming, heartbreaking tale of cute, ageless aliens hunting their lady, its dream houses with their tragic, magic guardians, and, as a show-stopping finale, its psychedelic love song.

With these stories *The Saga of the Swamp Thing* made comics history. Once you've read them, I think you'll understand why. So be prepared: prepare for blood and bad craziness, for Hell and dark water, for death. And be prepared also for trifles (as the Hystricide puts it), trifles light as air.

But even they have their darker side.

You'll find out.

— Neil Gaiman

World-renowned for The Sandman *and one of comics' most accomplished writers, Neil Gaiman is also the* New York Times *best-selling author of the novels* Anansi Boys, American Gods *and the Newbery Medal-winning* The Graveyard Book, *as well as the multimedia creations* Neverwhere, Stardust *and* Coraline. *Among his many awards are the Hugo, the Nebula, the Eisner, the Harvey, the Bram Stoker and the World Fantasy Award. Originally from England, Gaiman now lives in the United States.*

The Comics Code Authority was founded in 1954 by a number of publishers as a self-regulating body, following the outcry against comics (especially the E.C. line of horror comics) set in motion by the comic book witch-hunts of Dr. Frederic Wertham. The code forbade such elements as nudity, rotting zombies, incest and necrophilia, and the combination of these in "Love and Death" was far too rich for the people who administer the Code to handle. It is to DC's credit that, from this point on, rather than trying to tone down the title they chose to put it out without the Code's seal instead.

It was here that the artistic team really began to let loose. Bissette and Totleben give us insects that crawl between panel borders; Abigail Cable dragged into madness and beyond by her late uncle, crouched bloodied and beautiful in a corner; and a Swamp Thing who truly seems like part of the landscape.

(Inquisitive readers might like to know that Messrs. Moore, Bissette and Totleben can be seen in the library copy of *Deadlier Than the Male*, disposing of Young Tammy's remains.)

In "A Halo of Flies," Alfredo Alcala inked Steve Bissette's pencils. Alcala's artwork, if less detailed than Totleben's, is still moody, and reminiscent of old engravings. (An inker, incidentally, goes over a pencil artist's pencils in black ink, finishing the art and making reproduction easier — a good inker adds a great deal to the look, feel, and finish of the strip.)

"The Brimstone Ballet" effectively finishes the Arcane trilogy. Even though the overarching resolution does not occur until the following chapter, these three stories are obviously of a piece, sharing a mood, a bleakly unsettling, sometimes understated perspective of evil, of an approaching Armageddon, and how it affects a woman and her love. Rick Veitch pencilled this episode, allowing Steve Bissette to get a head start on the extra-length story that follows.

That story — "Down Amongst the Dead Men" from *Swamp Thing Annual* #2 — is a change of pace, and one of Moore's most popular Swamp Thing tales, something Moore himself feels has less to do with the story than the subject: What happens after we die?

His answer is classical, harking back to Dante's *The Divine Comedy*. He gives us an immediate afterlife zone of stunned, just-dead spirits and grazing poltergeists, as well as a Paradise — a small, beautiful, balmy place filled with the people one knew and loved. But, just as the most-read and remembered volume of *The Divine Comedy* is *The Inferno*, here the highest point is also the lowest: Hell. A Hades of gross demons, a place of tedium and pain.

While Dante Alighieri had Virgil and Beatrice as his guides, Swamp Thing's guided tour came from four displaced spirits — all of them long-established DC characters.

Deadman was once a circus aerialist named Boston Brand; murdered on the trapeze, he was granted the power to walk the earth whilst hunting his killer — a second chance given by an Oriental goddess named Rama Kushna, portrayed by artist Neal Adams as all eyes, lips, and Zipatone.

The man in the hat and cape is the Phantom Stranger, one of the most ambiguous of DC's characters. Who he is, where he comes from, and what his name is (if he has one) we have never been told. He's generally represented as some kind of agent of Cosmic Balance, appearing when necessary, then walking back into the shadows. Moore hints here at a history and nature for the Stranger that would seem to have begun well before the Fall.

The Spectre came to life — or death — in *More Fun Comics* fifty years ago, when policeman Jim Corrigan was murdered by gangsters. A mysterious light brought Corrigan back from the grave to fight crime as the Spectre. Over the years many different writers have handled the character, with varying takes on his powers, his size, his temper, and his relationship to Jim Corrigan. Here he is seen as some kind of guardian of the borders between Heaven and Hell.

Swamp Thing's final guide is the Demon, created by the man behind so much of what has been exciting in American comics: Jack Kirby, who drew inspiration for the look of the character from the battle mask worn by Hal Foster's *Prince Valiant*. We saw the Demon and his alter ego, Jason Blood (he of the candy-striped hair and the flared eyebrows), in the first *Swamp Thing* collection. Here we see him for the first time in his natural habitat.

These are horror stories: we watch the dead come back and discover the truth of the Black River and recorporations. We learn how to dance the Brimstone Ballet, and what the scariest thing in Arkham Asylum is on the scariest night in its history; and we find out who built Hell — and who builds it to this day.

So by this point, you'd think you would have a good idea of what to expect from *Swamp Thing*: dark messiahs, menaces to humanity, demons, nightmares.

And you'd be right. And you'd be wrong. Where the last three stories in this volume are concerned, at least, you'd be dead wrong.

As I mentioned earlier, sometimes fill-in artists have to step in, and with the amount of time that Bissette and Totleben needed to draw both "Down Amongst the Dead Men" in *Swamp Thing Annual* #2 and "Rite of Spring" in *The Saga of the Swamp Thing* #34, the stories in issues 32 and 33 both had to be fill-ins — but they are none the worse for it.

The first, "Pog," from *The Saga of the Swamp Thing* #32, is my personal favorite of all Alan Moore's Swamp Thing stories. It's a tribute to the work of cartoonist Walt Kelly and his creation, Pogo Possum.

Kelly began his career working for the Walt Disney Studios in the 1930s, and during World War Two he worked as a civilian employee for the army, producing artwork for language manuals. From 1948 to 1949 he was the art director for the short-lived but idealistic newspaper *The New York Star*, for whom he revived a character he had created earlier — Pogo — in the form of a daily comic strip by the same name. When the *Star* folded, *Pogo* went into syndication and was highly successful, lasting until Kelly's death in 1973.

Pogo Possum was part of an ensemble cast made up of inhabitants of the Okefenokee Swamp, scene of many a strange tale and pointed political satire. At a time when almost all other American newspaper strip creators were broadly conservative, Kelly was an unusual animal: a liberal, left-wing cartoonist who used his strip to discuss and parody such targets as the John Birch Society and the McCarthy hearings.

For some time, Moore had wanted to do a tribute in which the swamp-dwelling Pogo met the Swamp Thing. His chance came when he heard that Shawn McManus would be drawing one of the two upcoming fill-in issues. Moore knew that McManus's lighter style would be ideal for the book, as indeed it was.

One of the many delights of "Pog" is Moore's inventive use of language — what Lewis Carroll's Humpty Dumpty referred to as "portmanteau words": neologisms like "millenderings," containing in itself both "millennia" and "wanderings," or "guardiner," with overtones of both gardening and guardianship. This hodgepodge language is a joy to read, a tribute to the dialectical punmanship of Kelly's strip while still being uniquely Moore's. (As an aside, Alan maintains that once he had finished this issue, he found it difficult to write in normal English once more.)

Besides the use of guest artists, another option available to publishers when things are running late is to reprint previously published stories. *The Saga of the Swamp Thing* #33 was originally planned to be an all-reprint issue, but Moore successfully lobbied to add a framing sequence of new material around a single reprinted story. The final product, "Abandoned Houses," was written in a single day, and artist Ron Randall turned in a creditable art job on the shortest of notice.

"Abandoned Houses" is also a tribute, though full comprehension of all of its elements may require some rather esoteric background information.

It has long been a tradition in comics (one that goes back at least as far as E.C.'s

Introduction

It seems like a long time ago — swollen torrents of words have roared under many bridges; oceans of exotic imagery have swirled and risen; the shapes of continents have changed. Strange, how one's life passes. When I first read these stories, I was an aspiring comics writer who had barely begun to appreciate the skill and potential of the careful alchemical wedding of words and pictures which Alan Moore was daily practicing with love and dedication. Following a small but worthy tradition of adepts, Moore was working to transform the medium of his choice from what I, in common with many others, had regarded as an often cynically produced, pile-it-high, sell-it-cheap form of entertainment into something vital — something with currency.

I was always a slow learner. You can lead a horse to water but you can't make him drink — unless you hold his head under.

Rereading these stories for the first time, I am reminded how complacently adaptable humanity is as a species. Most change, we quickly learn to take for granted — short memories, a dangerous lack of vision, a lack of dangerous vision.

Some stories make a difference.

An adolescent poet once described Moore — with a touch of envy, perhaps — as having... purple orchids in his mind. Well, the heat and humidity of the Louisiana swamplands certainly brought them into full, gorgeous bloom and propagated them through the fertile imaginations and inkwells of Steve Bissette and John Totleben and others — to the lasting enrichment of all our lives.

I mentioned love (did I hear a rumor it was fashionable again?). Moore's and his collaborators' obvious love for and faith in their work is what seems to me to glow through these pages — most brightly vegetable, with the charming pathos of the respectful with "Pog" and the celebratory passion of "Rite of Spring," perhaps.

Arriving at "Rite of Spring" (the final story in this volume) seduced by the seeming ease of storytelling and command of the exigencies of serial plotting, we have sympathetically endured and enjoyed the horrors of the characters' lives as Moore gracefully allies us to their personal dramas. We have run the emotional gamut of demons, both terrifyingly crass and devilishly sophisticated, allowing our preconceptions to be disordered so that the mundane becomes exotic and the exotic mundane. Bewildered by the elegant rhythms of the prose and distracted by the ghastly delights of the illustration, we are left softened and raw, uncertain in a world both grotesque and deeply human — grotesquely human. We have been to Hell and

back — where will that stretched but warm and constant thread of human hope that tangles us and inextricably involves us in this madness lead us now? Into the maudlin pain and misery of irreconcilable and unrequited love? No, instead we are flung bodily into a vat, seething and bubbling with life's potent juices and held under until we breathe it in, absorbing — despite our disbelief, our cynicism — the revolutionary passion of the wild and impossible sexuality envisioned there.

But in comics nothing is impossible. It is proven in this story. Words unite with pictures in perfect complement. Love unites with horror; animal with vegetable; male with female; the natural with the supernatural. For a few brief pages we are given a tantalizing glimpse of what it might be like if we were big enough to realize all the possibilities of our myopic existences; if we were to find the way to truly embrace the mystery and begin "loving the alien." But that's another story — another dangerous vision.

Maybe I'm struggling with a difficult metaphor. Maybe it would just be simpler to say that anything that is made with love and imbued with hope is an inspiration that should not be taken for granted — that's the difference between art and craft. Lots of people can acquire the craft but the art has to be nurtured. You need to be able to feel it and believe it, to trust it, to have faith — and that's what comes through here.

Work such as some of that contained within this volume expanded the possibilities of the medium for others of us with lesser vision.

Sometimes it is easy to be lazy. Faith can become cynical almost without our noticing it — like growing hard skin.

Sometimes stories can make a difference — even old ones.

Thanks for that.

— Jamie Delano
Northampton
July 1990

Born in 1954, Jamie Delano has made a diverse, cross-genre contribution to the comic book medium, scripting — over some 25 years — both original works (World Without End, Tainted, Ghostdancing, Hell Eternal, Cruel and Unusual, Territory, Outlaw Nation) *and publisher-owned properties* (Captain Britain, Dr. Who, Night Raven, Hellblazer, Animal Man, Batman, Shadowman). *He is currently practicing for retirement, living in semi-rural England with his partner, Sue. They have three adult children and four grandchildren.*

Foreword

Love and Death — An Overture

The following foreword was originally written by Neil Gaiman between 1986 and 1987 as three separate introductions for the black and white Swamp Thing *collections published in England by Titan Books. An abridged version then appeared in the* Swamp Thing: Love and Death *trade paperback, first released by DC Comics in 1990. For this new hardcover edition we have expanded the piece to restore those abridged sections.*

Hi. Good to see you. Welcome to the swamp. Find somewhere relatively dry to sit, and I'll tell you about the stories you'll find in this volume — the second collection of DC's *The Saga of the Swamp Thing*.

In the first volume we saw the start of the Moore/Bissette/Totleben incarnation of the character; we saw Jason Woodrue's cracked attempt to save the Green (the communal undermind of the plant world) from humanity; and we saw the Monkey King, Kamara, who was Fear Incarnate.

This volume begins with a story called "The Burial," originally published in *The Saga of the Swamp Thing* #28.

It is easy to forget, seeing these stories preserved in bound volumes for posterity, that this was not how they originally appeared. Like the vast majority of American comic books, they were produced monthly: every thirty days, twenty-three pages of *Swamp Thing* script were written by Alan Moore, laid out and pencilled by Steve Bissette, and inked by John Totleben.

Any attempt to produce art on a schedule like that can run into problems. If an artist or writer gets behind, then there are two choices: either one skimps and turns in a fast but less than excellent job, or one completes what one is working on to the standard one is aiming for and risks blowing publication dates sky high, upsetting editors (in this case the exceptional Karen Berger), upsetting readers, and so forth.

To prevent this from happening it is not unusual in mainstream comics for "fill-in" artists to be employed to do stories outside the ongoing continuity, allowing the regular artists on the book to catch up. "The Burial" is the first of these in Moore's run.

By comparison with what has gone before in the first *Swamp Thing* collection, and with much of what will come afterward, "The Burial" seems lightweight — a recapping of Swamp Thing's origin, which was first told in DC's *Swamp Thing* #1 in 1972. "The Burial," however, is more than that. Alec Holland is put to rest in this issue, but that's not all that's buried. It's the end of an era: a celebration of and memorial to the original Len Wein and Berni Wrightson stories. This is the story that gave *The Saga of the Swamp Thing* the freedom to move on: the shaggy Bissette/Totleben creature, turning brown with the approach of autumn, stares at the smooth and root-laced Wrightson version, fresh out of the swamp, and we see how far we have come.

In their day, the Wein/Wrightson Swamp Thing stories were groundbreaking and remarkable works, and anything done with the characters afterwards had always been done in their shadow. This story, in more ways than one, laid that ghost to rest.

I can still remember the feeling of shock with which I read "Love and Death" — the first episode in the next sequence, the Arcane trilogy. This was the first comic-book horror I had seen that actually horrified me; I became hooked, discovering with amazement that comics had the same capacity to disturb and unsettle that the best prose and film had. Here Alan Moore takes a hard look at the fragility of human life. From the opening images of Abigail Cable (née Arcane), naked and bleeding from her hopeless attempt at cleansing, we are served a rich brew of a story — nasty stuff that tastes like your worst nightmares. It begins with Abigail Arcane, and the bad thing, and the bugs. And it ends... elsewhere.

"Love and Death" also made comics history, as, beginning with this issue, *The Saga of the Swamp Thing* became the first DC comic with newsstand distribution to go out on a monthly basis without the Comics Code Authority's seal of approval.

SWAMP THING
CREATED BY LEN WEIN AND BERNI WRIGHTSON
PLUT
PLUT
THE BURIAL
AN
ALAN MOORE WRITER
SHAWN McMANUS ARTIST
KAREN BERGER EDITOR
TATJANA WOOD COLORIST
JOHN COSTANZA LETTERER
PRESENTATION

HOW DEEP...?
HOW DEEP...DOES IT HAVE... TO BE? THE SOIL IS...WET... THE DIGGING... DIFFICULT...
PLUT
...AND I...HAVE BEEN DIGGING... FOR SUCH... A LONG... TIME...
IT LOOKS NICE IN AUTUMN, DOESN'T IT?

INCIDENTALLY, YOU'RE NOT LOOKING TOO BAD YOURSELF...
ISN'T THIS FUNNY, WHAT'S HAPPENING TO YOUR SKIN?
HAS IT HAPPENED BEFORE?
NO...
I WAS NOT... IN TOUCH... WITH THE SEASONS... BEFORE...
HMM.
ANYTHING DROPPED OFF YET?
UH...
OH, HEY, LOOK! WHAT'S THAT BIRD?
BLUE... HERON...
ABBY... THINGS ARE GOING... WELL WITH YOU?
OH, SO YOU NOTICED THE CHANGE?
LISTEN, I REALLY OUGHT TO APOLOGIZE... THE WAY I WAS ACTING A COUPLE OF WEEKS BACK.
ALL THAT HAND-WRITING AND STUFF...
YOU SHOULDN'T TAKE ANY NOTICE. IT'S THE WHITE HAIR... IT MAKES ME LOOK MORE DISTRAUGHT THAN I AM.
SO... YOU... AND MATT..?

ME AND MATT ARE FINE.
HE'S REALLY PICKED UP, Y'KNOW? HE DOESN'T JUST SIT AROUND ANYMORE, AND THE DRINKING'S STOPPED...
HE'S OUT LOOKING FOR A HOUSE FOR US. DID I TELL YOU THAT?
A HOUSE? NO.
THE MONEY... IS YOUR JOB...?
AT ELYSIUM LAWNS? OH, THAT'S TREMENDOUS, JUST THE WAY IT'S WORKING OUT AND EVERYTHING...
AFTER THAT INCIDENT WITH THE DEMON CREATURE, I THOUGHT IT WOULD ALL BE... WELL, I DON'T KNOW WHAT I THOUGHT.
BUT IT WAS AMAZING... THEY JUST EXPLAINED EVERYTHING AWAY AS "MASS-HYSTERIA," STUFF LIKE THAT...
...SO THE HOME'S JUST CARRYING ON AS NORMAL, WHATEVER "NORMAL" IS...
OH, SAY, I WAS MEANING TO ASK YOU...
HAVE YOU NOTICED HOW LONG IT'S TAKING FOR THE FLIES TO DIE OFF THIS YEAR?
OUR MOTEL IS FULL OF 'EM. I WONDERED IF IT WAS, I DUNNO, SOMETHING TO DO WITH THE GLASSHOUSE EFFECT, OR...
UH... ALEC?

ALEC?
WHAT, DID YOU SEE SOMETHING, OR...?
DON'T...KEEP... CALLING ME... ALEC!
I...
I'M SORRY, I...
I'M... NOT... ALEC HOLLAND...
ALEC HOLLAND... IS...DEAD...
PLUT

...BUT NOT BURIED.
PLUT
HOW DEEP...?
HOW DEEP...DO YOU NEED...TO BURY...THE PAST...
...BEFORE...IT WILL STAY...DEAD?
WHERE?
WHERE ARE YOU?
WHAT ARE YOU?

YOU'RE...NOT... HOLLAND!
I'M...NOT HOLLAND!
HOLLAND DIED...
...DIED...IN AN... EXPLOSION!
I HAVE...HIS CONSCIOUSNESS ...HIS MEMORIES...
...BUT HE... HE IS... DEAD...
I WILL... NOT...
...BE HAUNTED...
...BY MYSELF.

WAIT...
WAIT... DON'T GO...
COME BACK...
PLEASE...
PLEASE COME BACK...

BUT HE DIDN'T... COME BACK...
PLUT
AND SO I... HAD TO FOLLOW... HIM...
FOLLOW HIM... THROUGH THE LUMINOUS DUSK...
FOLLOW HIM... ALONG THE BRITTLE PATHS... OF AUTUMN...
THROUGH POOLS OF COLD WATER...
...FOLLOW HIM HERE.

HERE...
...WHERE IT BEGAN.
STILL STANDING, BUT BARELY...
NAKED ROOMS... FILTHY WITH WET ASH...
...A SOILED SHRED OF UPHOLSTERY... ITS FADED PATTERN... ONCE FAMILIAR...
HOME.
HEY, SKINNY...
DID YOU MAKE IT THIS MORNING?
WELL, YEAH, OF COURSE I...
THE BED? OH, YEAH... I MADE THE BED...
KNEW IT!
YOU NEVER TUCK IT IN PROPERLY ON MY SIDE.
I ALWAYS KNOW WHEN YOU'VE MADE IT. IT'S LIKE YOU'VE SIGNED THE QUILT IN THE BOTTOM RIGHT CORNER...
OH, GOD, THAT'S WORSE! LET ME DO IT...

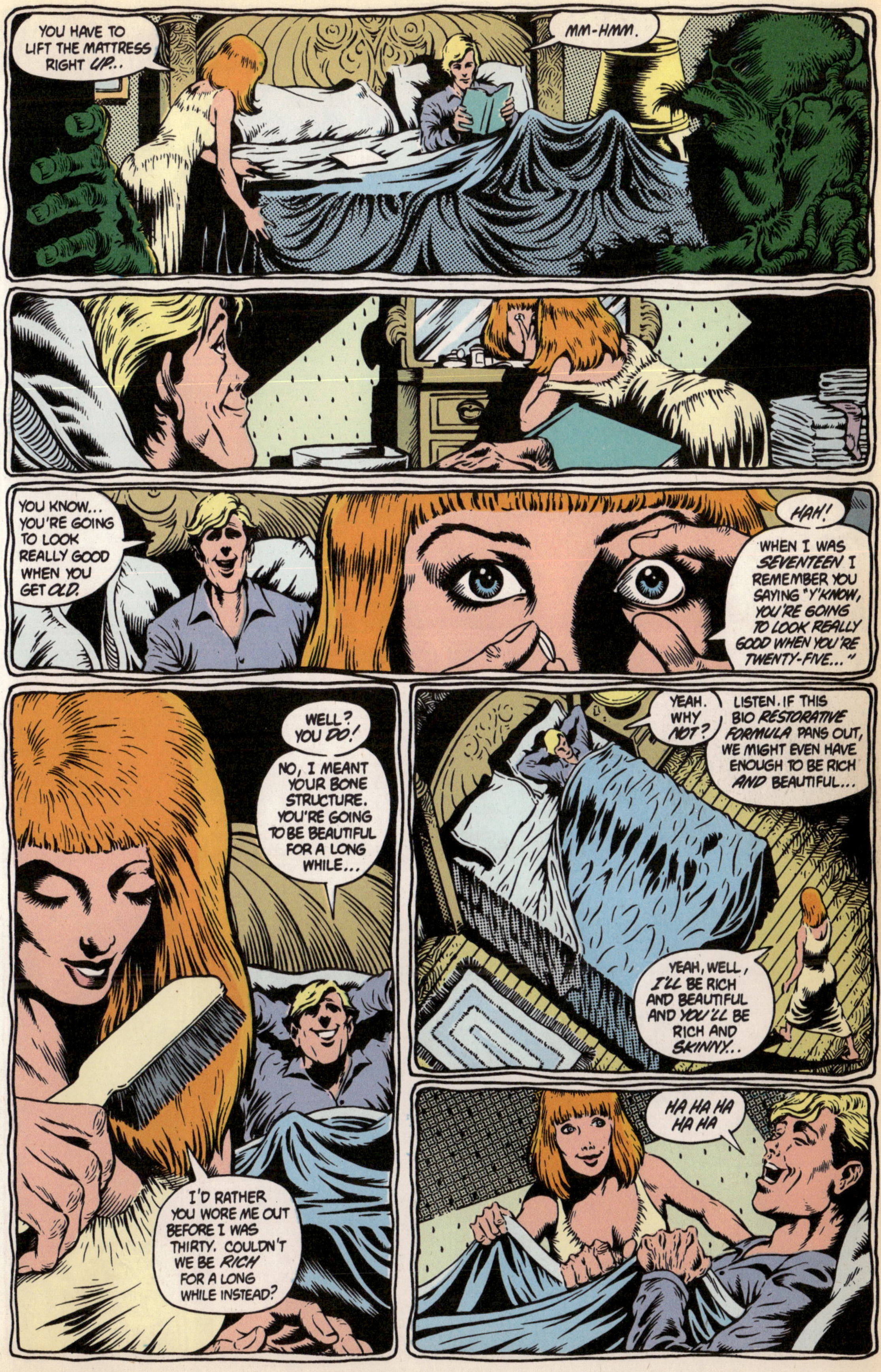
YOU HAVE TO LIFT THE MATTRESS RIGHT UP..
MM-HMM.
YOU KNOW... YOU'RE GOING TO LOOK REALLY GOOD WHEN YOU GET OLD.
HAH!
WHEN I WAS SEVENTEEN I REMEMBER YOU SAYING "Y'KNOW, YOU'RE GOING TO LOOK REALLY GOOD WHEN YOU'RE TWENTY-FIVE..."
WELL? YOU DO!
NO, I MEANT YOUR BONE STRUCTURE. YOU'RE GOING TO BE BEAUTIFUL FOR A LONG WHILE...
I'D RATHER YOU WORE ME OUT BEFORE I WAS THIRTY. COULDN'T WE BE RICH FOR A LONG WHILE INSTEAD?
YEAH. WHY NOT?
LISTEN. IF THIS BIO RESTORATIVE FORMULA PANS OUT, WE MIGHT EVEN HAVE ENOUGH TO BE RICH AND BEAUTIFUL...
YEAH, WELL, I'LL BE RICH AND BEAUTIFUL AND YOU'LL BE RICH AND SKINNY..
HA HA HA HA HA

YOU COLD?
NO.
ARE YOU READING?
NO...
HOME.
...WHERE THE HEART IS...
WHERE WE LIVED, ME...AND LINDA...
...WHERE WE DIED.
BUT, DR. HOLLAND... WE CAME TO YOU IN GOOD FAITH!

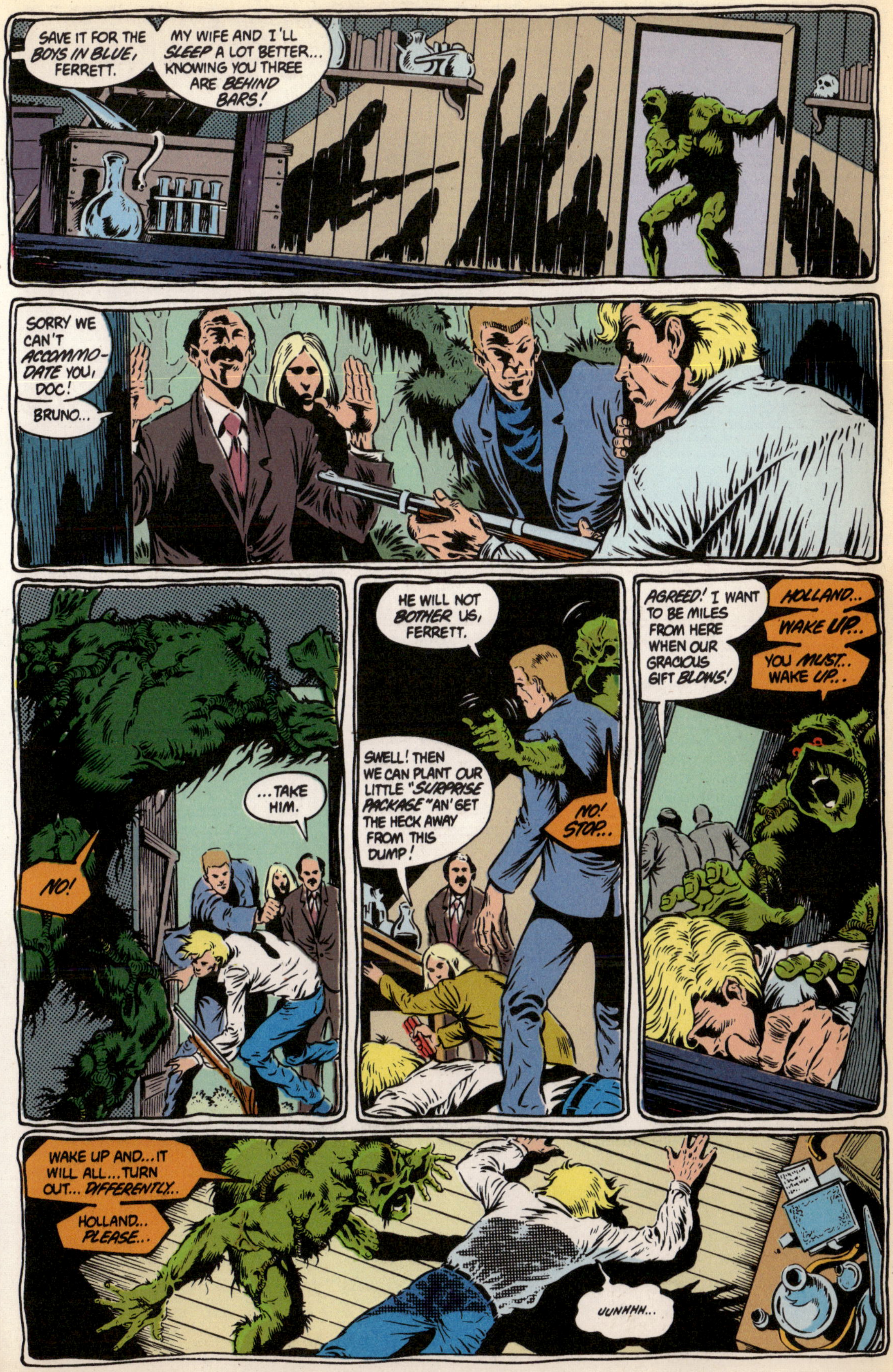
SAVE IT FOR THE BOYS IN BLUE, FERRETT.
MY WIFE AND I'LL SLEEP A LOT BETTER... KNOWING YOU THREE ARE BEHIND BARS!
SORRY WE CAN'T ACCOMMODATE YOU, DOC!
BRUNO...
...TAKE HIM.
NO!
HE WILL NOT BOTHER US, FERRETT.
SWELL! THEN WE CAN PLANT OUR LITTLE "SURPRISE PACKAGE" AN' GET THE HECK AWAY FROM THIS DUMP!
NO! STOP...
AGREED! I WANT TO BE MILES FROM HERE WHEN OUR GRACIOUS GIFT BLOWS!
HOLLAND...
WAKE UP...
YOU MUST... WAKE UP...
WAKE UP AND... IT WILL ALL... TURN OUT... DIFFERENTLY..
HOLLAND... PLEASE...
UUNHHH...

FEELS LIKE THEY DROPPED A *MOUNTAIN* ON MY HEAD! THEY'VE...
HEY, SEEMS MY PLAYMATES HAVE DECIDED TO *SKIP OUT!* I WONDER *WHY* THEY...
OH MY DEAR GOD.
THAT THING IS... *TICKING!*
GOTTA TRY...
...TO DEFUSE IT...
...BEFORE...
EEEEEEEEEEEEEEEEEEEEEEEE

EEEEEEEEEEEEEEEEEEEEEEEEEEEEEEEEEEEEEEEE
THERE...
IT IS DONE.
PLUT

ALL DONE.
BUT WHERE...
...IS THE BODY?
FOR HOURS I SAT...
...AND WATCHED...
...AND WAITED...
NOTHING.
ALMOST NOTHING.

ALMOST...
ALMOST NOTHING.

YOU...CAN SEE ME...?
HEAR ME...?
BUT... I HAVE SO MUCH ...TO TELL YOU...
YOUR FUTURE...
THINGS... THAT YOU... MUST KNOW...
THE MUD...?
SOMETHING... UNDER... THE MUD?

NOTHING.
AN EMPTY SPACE... MAKES EMPTY GESTURES...
...AND I HAVE DUG... AN EMPTY GRAVE...
...TO FIT... A VANISHED BODY.

BUT THAT...IS WHAT ...YOU WERE TRYING... TO TELL ME, ISN'T IT...?
THE BODY... DIDN'T...VANISH...
THE MIND...
IT WAS...THE MIND...THAT VANISHED...
...VANISHED...INTO THE GREENERY... THAT ABSORBED... THE SPOILED FLESH...
...CREATING A NEW ORGANISM...
CREATING ME.
THE MIND VANISHED...
...AND THE FLESH VANISHED...
...BUT THE BONES... REMAINED...

...DOWN HERE... IN THE COLD...
...ALL THOSE... DARK YEARS...
YOU MUST...
...HAVE BEEN...
...LONELY...
COME...
I HAVE... PREPARED...A PLACE FOR YOU...
LET US HOPE...
...THAT IT IS... DEEP ENOUGH...

PLUT
THERE.
BUT...THERE IS...NO MARKER.
CHRREK!

HE'S THERE...
I KNOW... THAT HE... IS THERE...
AND I KNOW... THAT HE... IS SMILING...
... BUT I DON'T... LOOK BACK.
next: Love and DEATH!

DC
The SAGA of the
SWAMP THING
75¢
29
OCT. 84
BY
ALAN MOORE,
STEPHEN BISSETTE
AND JOHN TOTLEBEN

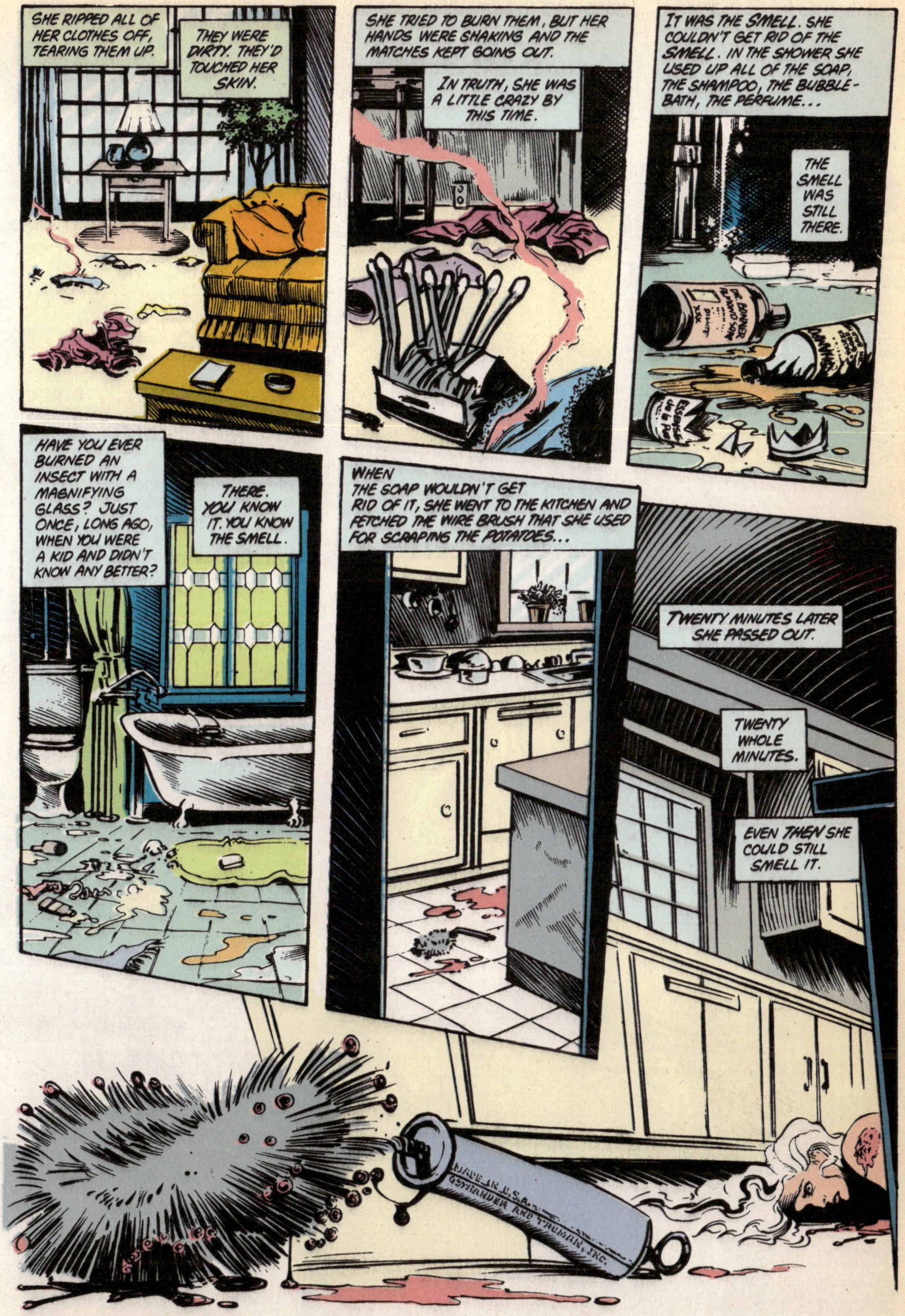
SHE RIPPED ALL OF HER CLOTHES OFF, TEARING THEM UP.
THEY WERE DIRTY. THEY'D TOUCHED HER SKIN.
SHE TRIED TO BURN THEM, BUT HER HANDS WERE SHAKING AND THE MATCHES KEPT GOING OUT.
IN TRUTH, SHE WAS A LITTLE CRAZY BY THIS TIME.
IT WAS THE SMELL. SHE COULDN'T GET RID OF THE SMELL. IN THE SHOWER SHE USED UP ALL OF THE SOAP, THE SHAMPOO, THE BUBBLE-BATH, THE PERFUME...
THE SMELL WAS STILL THERE.
HAVE YOU EVER BURNED AN INSECT WITH A MAGNIFYING GLASS? JUST ONCE, LONG AGO, WHEN YOU WERE A KID AND DIDN'T KNOW ANY BETTER?
THERE. YOU KNOW IT. YOU KNOW THE SMELL.
WHEN THE SOAP WOULDN'T GET RID OF IT, SHE WENT TO THE KITCHEN AND FETCHED THE WIRE BRUSH THAT SHE USED FOR SCRAPING THE POTATOES...
TWENTY MINUTES LATER SHE PASSED OUT.
TWENTY WHOLE MINUTES.
EVEN THEN SHE COULD STILL SMELL IT.
MADE IN U.S.A.
OSTRANDER AND TRUMAN, INC.

SHE COULD SMELL IT IN HER DREAMS.
SWAMP THING
CREATED BY LEN WEIN and BERNI WRIGHTSON
THE DREAM HAD STARTED OUT SO NICELY...
SHE WAS OUT IN THE SWAMP, AND HE WAS THERE, AND THEY WERE FRIENDS AGAIN...
HELLO.
HELLO... ABBY.
IT... HAS BEEN... A LONG TIME.
I MISSED YOU.
I THOUGHT...

LOVE AND DEATH
ALAN MOORE WRITER
STEPHEN BISSETTE and JOHN TOTLEBEN ARTISTS
KAREN BERGER EDITOR
TATJANA WOOD COLORIST
JOHN COSTANZA LETTERER
WELL, YOU KNOW, AFTER THE LAST TIME I SAW YOU...
I THOUGHT YOU DIDN'T LIKE ME ANYMORE.
I'M SORRY... I KNOW I MADE YOU MAD, I KEPT CALLING YOU ALEC, AND I KNOW THAT YOU'RE NOT ALEC, BUT...
I CAN'T GET USED TO CALLING YOU ANYTHING ELSE. I'M SORRY, I'M AN IDIOT, I KNOW, BUT...
ABBY...
IT DOESN'T MATTER.
NOT ANY MORE.

YOU CAN CALL ME ALEC... IF IT'S EASIER...

I CAN?
OH, GOD, I THOUGHT YOU HATED ME. I THOUGHT JUST WHEN THINGS WERE GOING RIGHT FOR ME, I WAS GOING TO LOSE YOU. OH, ALEC, I...
AND THEN THEY WERE BOTH LAUGHING.
AND THEN SHE HUGGED HIM, AND HE HUGGED HER BACK AND SHE COULDN'T BREATHE BUT THAT WAS OKAY...
HE WHIRLED HER AROUND, AND HER FEET WERE NO LONGER TOUCHING THE GROUND. SHE BURIED HER FACE IN HIS CHEST AND BREATHED IN A SCENT OF LIFE AND LOAM AND AUTUMN.
IT SMELLED GOOD.
NOT LIKE THIS.
NOT LIKE THIS AT ALL.

THE DREAM TWISTED THEN, FOLDING IN UPON ITSELF AND BLOSSOMING INTO NEW SHAPES.
THE LIGHT CHANGED, AS IF A CLOUD OF BLOWFLIES HAD SUDDENLY OBSCURED THE SUN...
...AND SHE WAS WITH HER HUSBAND, AND HE SAID HE HAD THREE SURPRISES FOR HER.
OH, MATT, COME ON! WHAT?
GUESS.
YOU'VE DISCOVERED YOU'RE HEIR TO THE THRONE OF DUBROVNIA?
NOPE.
YOU'VE JOINED THE MOONIES.
UH-UH.
YOU'RE REALLY ALLEN FUNT AND FOR THE PAST THREE YEARS I'VE BEEN ON CANDID CAMERA.
CLOSE, BUT NO CIGAR.
I WANT A DIVORCE.
FAIR ENOUGH. BUT YOU'LL BE SO-REE.
MATT, IF YOU DON'T TELL ME WHAT THIS SURPRISE IS, YOU'LL BE CHAIRBOUND!
GMJ
OH, OKAY, IF YOU'RE GOING TO GET VIOLENT...
YOU WANT TO KNOW WHAT THE SURPRISE IS?
WELL, WE'RE RIGHT NOW PARKED OUTSIDE OF IT.
WE'RE...?

NICE PLACE, HUH?
I PUT A DOWN PAYMENT ON IT YESTERDAY.
WANT TO TAKE A LOOK INSIDE?
C'MON...
IK...
ONE FOOT IN FRONT OF THE OTHER...
SEE? IT'S EASY...

AND SO THEY'D GONE INSIDE.
INSIDE, IT LOOKED EVEN BETTER.
MATT... ALL THIS FURNITURE! THESE CARPETS...
THEY CAME WITH THE HOUSE. THE PEOPLE WHO OWNED THIS PLACE DIDN'T WANT THE TROUBLE AND EXPENSE OF MOVING THEM, I GUESS.
COME ON... LET'S LOOK AROUND...
THE LIVING ROOM...
THE KITCHEN...
THE DREAM WAVERED HERE. HERE WAS WHERE THE BAD THING WAS HIDDEN... A SUDDEN SCENT OF SMOLDERING INSECT FLESH, ACRID AND BITTER BEHIND THE NOSTRILS...
BEDROOM...
...AND THEN IT WAS GONE.
MATT? HOW DID YOU FIND THIS PLACE? WE CAN'T AFFORD ANYTHING LIKE THIS!
WE ONLY HAVE MY JOB AT ELYSIUM LAWNS...
THAT'S MY SECOND SURPRISE.
COME ON... BACK TO THE CAR.
ALMOST GONE.

ALMOST.

TENTATIVE FEELERS BRUSHED AGAINST THE SKIN OF HER DELIRIUM. THERE WAS THE BEATING OF MINIATURE WINGS. THERE WERE ARMS WITH TWO ELBOWS...
HERE...
HERE WAS WHERE THE BAD THING HAD REALLY STARTED...
WELL? WE'RE HERE. WHAT DO YOU THINK OF IT?
WHAT DO I THINK OF WHAT?
WHAT DO YOU THINK OF THE PLACE WHERE I WORK?
BLACKRIVER RECORPORATIONS
WHERE YOU WORK?
YOU HAVE A JOB?
MATTHEW! MATTHEW, M'BOY!
ERIC!
ABBY, THIS IS ERIC LOVEDAY. ERIC'S MY BOSS.
ERIC, THIS IS MY WIFE, ABIGAIL.
A LOVELY NAME FOR A LOVELY YOUNG WOMAN.
COME ON INSIDE, ABBY, AND MEET THE WHOLE SICK CREW...
NO. NOT INSIDE. DON'T GO INSIDE. THE SMELL WAS WORSE INSIDE...

OFFICE
INSIDE, JUST FOR A MOMENT, SHE HAD SEEN WHERE THE SMELL WAS COMING FROM.
EVERYBODY'S THROUGH HERE, ABIGAIL.
YOU KNOW THE WAY YOUR HUBBY HERE GOT HIS JOB... HEH...
DIDJA TELL HER, MATTHEW?
I THOUGHT I'D LEAVE IT TO YOU, ERIC. YOU TELL IT BETTER.
MATTHEW HERE WAS DRIVING BY, ABOUT A WEEK BACK NOW. NOTICES THE PLACE FOR THE FIRST TIME, THINKS "HMM. GUESS I'LL TAKE A LOOK!"
HEH. THIS NEXT BIT IS FUNNY...
I WAS EXPECTING SOMEBODY FROM A JOB AGENCY, FILL A VACANCY WE HAD, RIGHT? SO, I SEE MATTHEW PULL UP, I STORM STRAIGHT ON OUT THERE...
"HEY! YOU! DO YOU REALIZE YOU'RE AN HOUR LATE?"
SO THEN MATTHEW HERE, HE SAYS...
EXCUSE ME A MOMENT, ERIC...
ABBY? ABBY, ARE YOU ALL RIGHT?
UH... FINE... I, UH, JUST SUCH A SURPRISE, I...
UH...
FETCH ABBY SOME COFFEE, ERIC.
RIGHT AWAY, MATTHEW...

THE COFFEE CAME, AND SHE DRANK IT, AND EVERYTHING WAS ORDINARY.
SHE MET GUS PRITCHETT, WHO HANDLED INVOICING, AND BETTY MONTCLAIR, WHO COULDN'T MOVE HER FACE BECAUSE OF A STROKE...
SHE MET SALLY PARKS, WHOSE NAME SOUNDED FAMILIAR, AND MARK NEWELL, A PRETTY OFFICE JUNIOR WHO BLUSHED WHEN HE SHOOK HER HAND...
...THE WHOLE SICK CREW.
...AND THEN SHE AND MATT WERE OUTSIDE AGAIN, WALKING BACK TO THE CAR.
SHE DIDN'T TELL HIM WHAT SHE'D SEEN WHEN ERIC LOVEDAY OPENED THE DOOR.
HE DIDN'T TELL HER WHAT "RECORPORATIONS" MEANT.
...AND HER ONLY QUESTION WAS THE ONE SHE SHOULD NEVER HAVE ASKED.
MATT...YOU SAID THREE SURPRISES.
IT'LL PROBABLY MAKE ME GO DIZZY AGAIN, BUT WHAT'S THE THIRD SURPRISE?
OH, I THINK I'LL SAVE THAT ONE FOR LATER.
LET'S GO HOME.
HOME?

HOME.
IT WAS HER HOME AND SHE AND MATT OWNED IT AND IT WAS BEAUTIFUL. SHE WASN'T THINKING ABOUT ANYTHING ELSE.
WHY WASN'T SHE THINKING ABOUT ANYTHING ELSE?
AND MATT...
MATT HAD CHANGED SO MUCH. ALL THE WEAKNESS AND DESPAIR HAD GONE, LEAVING A NEW STRENGTH, AN UNFAMILIAR CONFIDENCE...
AND THEN THEY WENT INSIDE...
AND THEN THERE WAS...
NO.
AND THEN THERE WAS THE...
NO! IT DIDN'T HAPPEN!
...THE BAD THING.
YES.

SHE DIDN'T WANT TO THINK ABOUT IT, BUT THERE WAS THAT BUG-TASTE IN THE BACK OF HER MOUTH, AND...
NO.
SHE DUG HER HEELS INTO THE FLANKS OF HER NIGHTMARE AND MADE IT GO A DIFFERENT WAY...
AND THEN... JUST FOR A MOMENT... SHE WASN'T IN HER OWN DREAM ANYMORE.
SHE WAS IN SOMEONE ELSE'S DREAM.
HIS DREAM...
HE'D FOUND A BIRD, FALLEN IN BLACK GRASS THAT WAS SHARP ENOUGH TO CUT YOUR FINGER.
WRETCHED AND SMASHED, IT LAY LIKE A BLOODIED SHUTTLECOCK. IT WAS DEAD...
... BUT IT WAS MOVING.
WHY WAS IT MOVING?
HIS HAND REACHED OUT TO TOUCH IT. ITS EYES REGARDED HIM, MILKY AND OPAQUE...
...THEN SOMEONE DROPPED A DARK AND POLISHED STONE INTO HER DREAMPOOL, SHATTERING THE IMAGE WITH RIPPLES LIKE CONJURERS' HOOPS...
... AND THE SMELL WAS EVERYWHERE.

EVEN WHEN SHE'D GONE OVER TO THE LIBRARY IN HOUMA, WHERE NOTHING STRANGE EVER HAPPENED AND REALITY WAS ALPHABETICALLY FILED...
EVEN THERE.
TERREBONNE PARISH PUBLIC LIBRARY
NO PARKING ANY TIME
EXCUSE ME?
IS THERE A SECTION WHERE YOU KEEP YOUR PSYCHOLOGY BOOKS?
PSYCHOLOGY OR PSYCHIATRY?
UH... WELL, I DON'T KNOW... I'M WORKING WITH AUTISTIC KIDS AND I WAS LOOKING FOR...
PSYCHOLOGY. OVER IN THE FAR CORNER.
RIGHT.
THANKS.
THE SIEGE
CLARA CLAIBORNE PARK
THUK
THE PROFESSION OF VIOLENCE
OH
SSHHHHH!

DEADLIER THAN THE MALE
THE FACTS ABOUT SALLY PARKS
by DR. NILES RICHY
THE FACTS ABOUT SALLY PARKS
Introduction by J.P. SHANNON.
ILLUSTRATED WITH PHOTOS
PSYCHOLOGY
TTI!

SHE'D DRIVEN HOME (HOME?) WITH THE BOOK ON THE SEAT BESIDE HER, FACE DOWN.
WHEN SHE GOT BACK TO THE HOUSE, SHE READ IT, SKIMMING FRANTICALLY.
IT WAS ALL ABOUT SALLY PARKS WHOSE NAME HAD SOUNDED FAMILIAR.
SALLY PARKS, WHO, IN THE LAST THREE MONTHS OF HER TWENTY-SIX BRIEF YEARS, HAD DONE MANY INTERESTING AND NOTABLE THINGS.
DECIPHER THE MALE
SHE HAD KILLED FIFTEEN PEOPLE...
(EMPLOYER, EMPLOYER'S WIFE AND TEENAGE DAUGHTER, HER OWN BOY-FRIEND, HER BOYFRIEND'S MOTHER, TWO POLICE OFFICERS, ONE NEWSBOY...)
...WITH A VARIETY OF WEAPONS...(GUN, LETTER OPENER, TIRE-IRON, WIRE COAT HANGER...)
...FOR NO REASON AT ALL... ...BEFORE BEING SHOT DEAD BY POLICE ON THE NIGHT OF AUGUST 7TH, 1962.
THAT SALLY PARKS.
The bodies of Young Tammy
from the scene of the first
Sally Parks was
...WHO, TWENTY-TWO YEARS LATER, HAD A NICE LITTLE JOB TYPING MEMOS FOR BLACKRIVER RECORPORATIONS, INC.
WHY HADN'T SHE ASKED?
WHY HADN'T SHE ASKED WHAT "RECORPORATIONS" MEANT?

WHAT ABOUT THE REST OF THEM? BETTY MONTCLAIR? WAS SHE DEAD, TOO?
ERIC LOVEDAY?
GUS PRITCHETT?
MARK NEWELL?
MATT?
THE SHADOWS OF THE ROOM BEGAN TO SPIRAL AND WHIRLPOOL AND SHE CLUTCHED DESPERATELY AT HER TRAIN OF THOUGHT, A BLACK THREAD IN A BLACKER LANDSCAPE.
MATT. MATT WAS HER HUSBAND.
HE JUST DIDN'T ACT LIKE HER HUSBAND. HE HUNG AROUND WITH DEAD PEOPLE AND PULLED JOBS AND HOUSES OUT OF NOWHERE. HE WAS DIFFERENT.
HOW LONG HAD HE BEEN DIFFERENT?
HE'D BEEN DIFFERENT SINCE THE NIGHT OF THE TROUBLE UP AT ELYSIUM LAWNS, THE NIGHT THEY'D ARGUED...
BUT EVEN BEFORE THAT... SINCE THEY WERE IN WEST VIRGINIA, IN FACT...
WHAT HAD HAPPENED IN...
... WEST VIRGINIA?
FROM DEEP INSIDE HER, THE BAD THING STARTS TO CRAWL TOWARD THE LIGHT...
...AND SHE KNOWS.

SHE KNOWS WHAT RECORPORATIONS ARE.
SHE KNOWS WHICH BLACK RIVER, HEADING WHERE...
BLACKRIVER RECORPORATIONS
AND WHY THE DEAD BIRD MOVES...
...AND WHO LOOKS OUT FROM BEHIND HER HUSBAND'S EYES.
THE SMELL THE BURNING ANT HILL STENCH OF IT...
HIS NAME SLAMS INTO HER MIND, AND HER KNEES BUCKLE BEFORE ITS AWFUL FORCE.
HIS NAME, A SIGNATURE SCRAWLED IN ACID...
AND SHE THINKS "HOW LONG HAVE I BEEN MARRIED TO...?"
AND SHE THINKS "HOW MANY TIMES DID...?"
AND SHE KNOWS WHAT THE BAD THING IS, AND WHERE THE STENCH IS COMING FROM.

IT'S HER...
UUEEEEEIIGHHH
...AND SHE CANNOT TEAR THE CONTAMINATION AWAY FROM HER...
...OR BURN IT...
...OR SMOTHER IT WITH PERFUME...
...OR SCRAPE IT FROM HER SKIN...
AND HER DREAMS ARE REEKING, UNBEARABLE THINGS...

...AND HER WAKING IS NO RELIEF.
OH GOD...
CLOTHES...
WHERE DID I PUT... UUEUUGH...
...FIND MY CLOTHES...
GET OUT...
GET OUT GET OUT GET OUT.
GET OUT QUICK...
GET OUT QUICK BEFORE...

HELLO, HON.
HOPE YOU DON'T MIND...
... BUT I BROUGHT SOME FRIENDS HOME.
OH... UHHHH...
NO! NO, COME IN!
I, UH, I, UH, OUGHTA GO TO THE STORE... GET SOMETHING FOR DINNER...
OH, DON'T WORRY ABOUT THAT, ABIGAIL.
WE'LL TAKE YOU AS WE FIND YOU.
THAT'S RIGHT.
YOUR WIFE LOOKS NERVOUS, MATTY...
HMM. YES, YOU'RE RIGHT.
WHAT IS IT, AB? WHAT'S THE MATTER, SOMETHING ON YOUR MIND?
I...I KNOW WHO YOU ARE! I...
OH GOD...
LOOK, PLEASE, WHAT DO YOU WANT ME TO SAY?
HHUHH...
WHAT DO WE WANT YOU TO SAY?
WELL, THAT'S EASY...
OH NO. NO. NO NO.

JUST SAY UNCLE.

HE REACHES OUT TOWARD THE BIRD.
IS IT STILL ALIVE? WHAT CAUSES IT TO WRITHE AND TWITCH...
...IF NOT LIFE?
BUGS!
HE SAW IT MOVE AND THOUGHT IT WAS ALIVE...
...BUT IT WAS FULL OF BUGS!
IT HAD BEEN FULL OF BUGS ALL THE TIME.
NEXT: "A HALO OF FLIES"

DC
The SAGA of the
SWAMP THING
75¢
30
NOV. 84
APPROVED BY THE COMICS CODE AUTHORITY
SR BISSETTE & TOTLEBEN

THE RETURNED MAN SMILES...
...AND OUTSIDE THE LOUISIANA SKY SOARS FROM RIM TO RIM, CURDLING THE NOVEMBER CLOUDS.
THE RETURNED MAN CHUCKLES...
...AND A SHOCKWAVE OF NIGHTMARE RIPPLES OUT ACROSS THE SLEEPING CONTINENT...
...AND IN LAFAYETTE, JODY HERBERT COMES ACROSS THE WINO PASSED OUT IN AN ALLEYWAY AND JODY HAS A BOOK OF MATCHES IN HIS POCKET AND THERE'S NOBODY ELSE AROUND...
...AND IN ALEXANDRIA, TINA-LOUISE PIERCE SAYS "THE HELL WITH IT" AND LIFTS THE ANCIENT IRON FRYING PAN THAT HER HUSBAND IS TOO CHEAP TO REPLACE...

...AND IN SHREVEPORT, JIM AND CAROLE PATTERSON'S PET CAT SPOCK DECIDES THAT THEIR SON RICKIE'S CRIB IS A WARM PLACE TO SIT...
...AND IN LAKE CHARLES A GUIDE DOG SUDDENLY GROWS IRRITATED WITH ITS MISTRESS...
...AND ON A FARM THREE MILES WEST OF CROWLEY, SOMETHING TERRIBLE IS BORN THAT CRIES LIKE A WOMAN AND THEN DIES...
...AND IN HOUMA, ABIGAIL CABLE JUST CAN'T STOP SCREAMING...
...AND THE RETURNED MAN LOOKS UPON HIS WORKS...
...AND HE SEES THAT THEY ARE GOOD.

A HALO OF FLIES
an
ALAN MOORE
WRITER
STEPHEN BISSETTE
and
ALFREDO ALCALA
ARTISTS
KAREN BERGER
EDITOR
TATJANA WOOD
COLORIST
JOHN COSTANZA
LETTERER
presentation

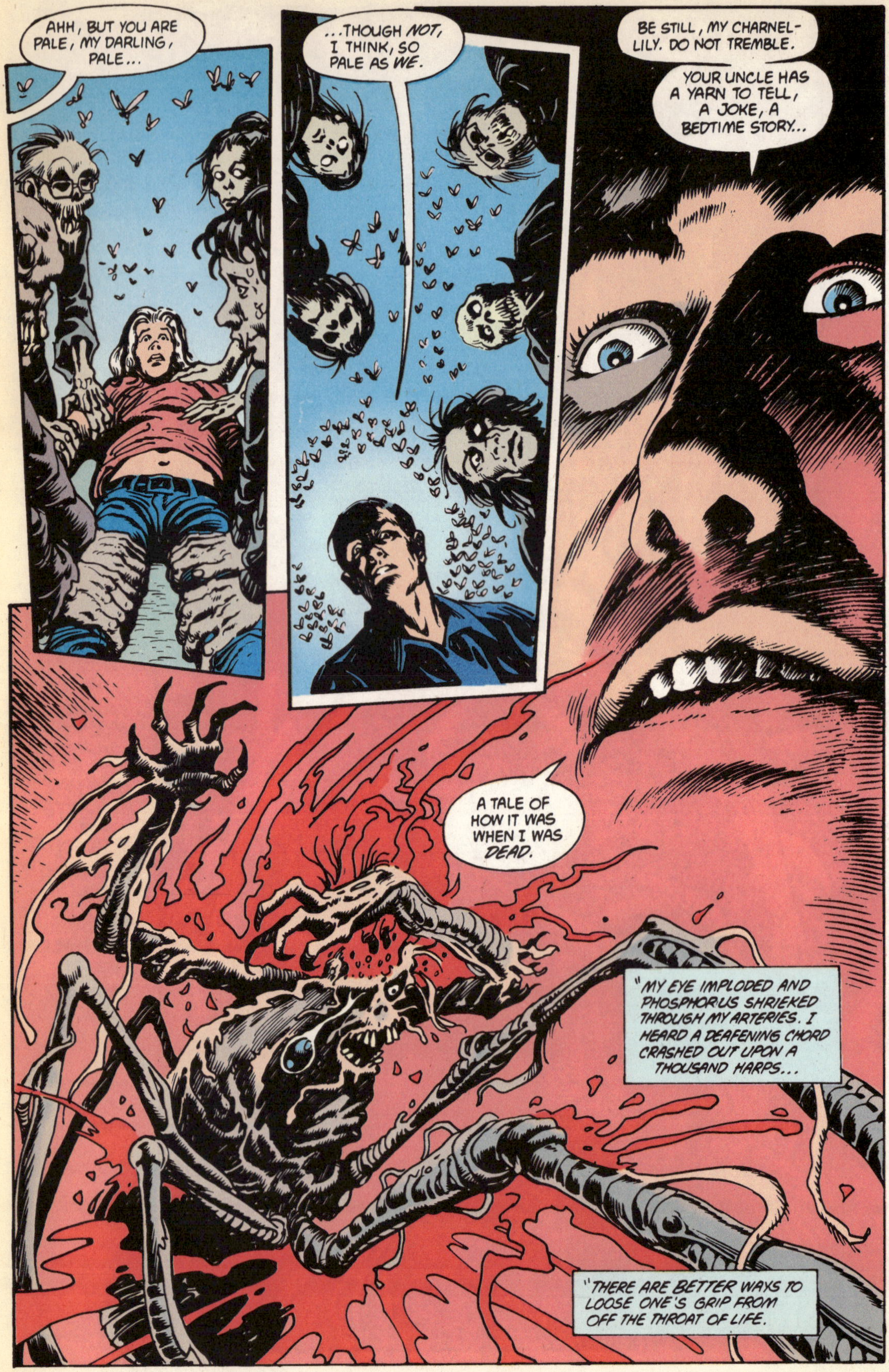
AHH, BUT YOU ARE PALE, MY DARLING, PALE...
...THOUGH NOT, I THINK, SO PALE AS WE.
BE STILL, MY CHARNEL-LILY. DO NOT TREMBLE.
YOUR UNCLE HAS A YARN TO TELL, A JOKE, A BEDTIME STORY...
A TALE OF HOW IT WAS WHEN I WAS DEAD.
"MY EYE IMPLODED AND PHOSPHORUS SHRIEKED THROUGH MY ARTERIES. I HEARD A DEAFENING CHORD CRASHED OUT UPON A THOUSAND HARPS...
"THERE ARE BETTER WAYS TO LOOSE ONE'S GRIP FROM OFF THE THROAT OF LIFE.

"IT WAS MY FAILURE THAT SHRIVELED ME. NEXT TO THIS, THE SCALDING EMBRACE OF THE LIGHTNING WAS AS NOTHING.
"WHILE REACHING FOR ANOTHER'S FLESH IN WHICH TO DRAPE MY INTELLECT, I HAD BEEN CHEATED!
"CHEATED BY A PAWN, A CYPHER, A THING NO MORE SIGNIFICANT THAN THE MOST DESPISED OF BEETLES...
"THIS BUG, THIS WORTHLESS SPECK, HAD WITH HIS DEATH DISPLACED DEATHLESS ARCANE...
"CONDEMNING ME TO THE DUSK LATITUDES...
"...TO THE COBWEBBED LANDS...

"...TO THE DISMAL REGION OF THE BODILESS MEN.

"THERE WERE SO MANY OF THEM, CAUGHT THERE IN THE FOGS OF AFTERLIFE, THEIR SOULS TOO DENSE AND IRONBOUND TO CLIMB TOWARD THE LIGHT.
"POISONERS, TRAITORS, TYRANTS AND TORTURERS...
"THEIR EVIL WAS MASSIVE. IT HAD A GRAVITY, A COLD PSYCHIC UNDERTOW THAT DRAGGED AT MY AWARENESS...
"BUT I STRUGGLED FREE, FROM FINGERS WITHOUT BLOOD OR BONE OR SINEW...
"STRUGGLED FREE FROM THAT MALIGN AND TREACLE-BLACK TWILIGHT...
"...MAKING MY WAY BACK TO THE BLEACHED HEMISPHERES BEYOND...
"...BACK TO MY DISCARDED CLAY AS A SERPENT WILL RETURN TO FRESH SLOUGHED SKIN.
"IT LAY THERE IN THE DIRT.
"SO SMALL...
"SO DIMINISHED...

"IT WAS A THING OF STARING, IDIOT SOCKETS AND SCORCHED METAL; OF MELTED WIRES THAT TRAILED LIKE GANGLIA FROM THE PERISHED FLESH.
"I COULD NOT WEAR THIS TRAVESTY.
"BUT I WAS IN THE WORLD ONCE MORE, THE WORLD THAT STRETCHED ABOUT ME LIKE A VAST WARDROBE, FILLED WITH HALF-AWAKE CORPSES.
"I WOULD CLOTHE MY SPIRIT ELSEWHERE..."
...IN WHATEVER RAGS WERE AVAILABLE.
YOU...
...TOOK MATT'S BODY... MADE HIM INTO A MONSTER...
OH GOD, MATT...
DEAREST ABIGAIL, YOUR GRASP OF THE INHUMAN IS SO LIMITED AND SHALLOW.
YOU SPARE YOURSELF THE FULLEST HORROR...
LONG BEFORE HE LOANED HIS FLESH TO ME, MATTHEW JOSEPH CABLE WAS NO STRANGER TO MONSTROSITY...

"WITH HIM, IT WAS A MONSTROSITY OF LUST, OF ABERRATIONS NURTURED AND WEAKNESSES INDULGED.
"A FLUKE OF THE BRAIN HAD GIVEN YOUR HUSBAND ABILITIES TO SHAKE WHAT GODS THERE BE, THE POWER TO BEND THE WORLD AND MAKE DREAMS TOUCHABLE.
"HE SQUANDERED IT ON TRIVIAL AND SQUALID DIORAMAS."
TROUTSKINNED WOMEN WITH THE LUSTER OF NEON...
...WOMEN OF SMOKE...
...MANIKINS TEXTURED LIKE APRICOTS...
NO!! I'M NOT LISTENING!! NO NO NO NO...
YESSSS!!
CERTAINLY, MY PROXIMITY DID NOT HINDER HIS DISINTEGRATION...
...BUT MATTHEW CABLE BEAT HIS OWN PATH TO HELL.
"I MERELY WAITED...
"...AND WATCHED...

"LENDING MY INFLUENCE TO AN OCCASIONAL DIVERSION...
"... A MOMENTARY DISTRACTION...
"... A CHOREOGRAPHED DISASTER.
"THE FINAL BLOW, WHEN STRUCK, CAME AS A STROKE OF SWEETEST MERCY.
"HE SURRENDERED HIS FLESH WILLINGLY..."
...AND WITHOUT REMORSE.

THUS, YOUR HUSBAND'S SHELL IS MINE TO WEAR...
...YOUR HUSBAND'S TALENTS MINE TO EMPLOY.
I AM ARCANE!
I AM RETURNED FROM THE DEAD..
...AND THERE IS NOTHING THAT I CANNOT DO.
AND THE RETURNED MAN SMILES...

...AND IN MONROE, HATTIE DUPLANTIS REMEMBERS HOW HER SISTER DOREEN (NOW SICK AND QUITE HELPLESS) USED TO TORMENT HER WHEN SHE WAS A CHILD...
...AND IN LITTLE ROCK, CHERYL AND LONI WILLIAMS WAIT UNTIL THEIR FATHER AND THEIR SLUTTY NEW STEPMOTHER ARE ASLEEP BEFORE PLAYING WITH THE KITTEN HE BOUGHT HER...
...AND IN BEAUMONT ALL THE TROPICAL FISH AT THE FIRST WATER PET SHOP BEGIN TO EAT, FIRST EACH OTHER, THEN THEMSELVES...
...AND IN SPRINGFIELD THERE IS A BRIEF AND SPECTACULAR PLAGUE OF LADYBUGS...
...AND BENEATH THE EARTH THERE ARE MUFFLED, BOOMING VOICES...
...AND BENEATH THE OCEAN THERE ARE TERRIBLE LIGHTS...

...AND ABOVE THE SKY A WATCHMAN WATCHES...
MONITOR...?
I THINK SOMETHING'S HAPPENING IN LOUISIANA...
I'M GETTING A WAVE-PORTRAIT AROUND THE EIGHT HUNDREDS...
THE EIGHT HUNDREDS? LET ME SEE...
HM.
ABOVE SIX HUNDRED WE'RE DEALING WITH POWER-USERS IN THE SUPERNATURAL CATEGORY...
ABOVE EIGHT HUNDRED WE'RE DEALING WITH EITHER THE DEMON TRIGON OR THE SPECTRE.
BOTH OF THOSE ARE CURRENTLY BEYOND THIS CONTINUUM, SIR...
YES. I KNOW.
IT'S SPREADING, WHATEVER IT IS... COVERING THE SOUTH AND HEADING NORTH...
TRIGON
WHAT SHOULD WE DO?
DO?
WE WATCH...
...AND THE RIPPLES WIDEN ACROSS AMERICA, SHIMMERING LIKE LIQUID CHROMIUM THROUGH THE VERY DARKEST MINDS... THE DESPERATE... THE DEPRAVED...

...THE DERANGED.
C'MON, WOODRUE, EASY, NOW...
...THE BAYOU...
...COMING OUT OF THE BAYOU...
WHAT THE HELL IS WRONG WITH THEM ALL TONIGHT?
RKHAM
SYLUM
R THE
ALLY
SANE
BEATS ME. WOODRUE JUST WENT BERSERK AND STARTED UP WHACKIN' HIS HEAD AGAINST THE CELL DOOR...
TROUBLE IS, ANATOMY LIKE THAT, WHO CAN SAY HOW BAD HE'S HURT HIMSELF?
HOW DO THEY EXPECT US TO COPE WITH FREAKS LIKE THESE?
I HAD TO HELP SEDATE TWO-FACE EARLIER. JEEZ, THAT GUY SCARES ME...
OH YEAH? YOU WANNA SEE SOMETHING REALLY SCARY?
THERE...
...THE JOKER'S STOPPED LAUGHING.
...AND THE WAVES ROLL OUT, SWELLING UPON A FEVER-TIDE, THEIR BLACKNESS UNRELIEVED BY FOAM...

...AND THE RETURNED MAN GESTURES WITH A STOLEN HAND...
...AND DISMISSES HIS SERVANTS...
...AND THEN GOES OUT...
...GOES OUT WALKING...
...SHIRTLESS IN THE FREEZING FOG.
AND AFTER A WHILE, IT BEGINS TO SNOW.

SWAMP THING
CREATED BY LEN WEIN and BERNI WRIGHTSON

HOLLAND...

MATT...?
MATTHEW CABLE NO LONGER EXISTS.
GUESS AGAIN.
ARCANE.
ARCAAAANE!

I AM RETURNED...
...AND THE ENERGIES THAT CHURN WITHIN ME ARE AS LIMITLESS...
...AS MY VERY GREAT NEED FOR REVENGE.
THEN WHY... DOES ONE...SO POWERFUL... WASTE... SO MUCH TIME... WITH TALK?
BECAUSE YOUR EVENTUAL DESTRUCTION IS ALREADY A FACT, ACCOMPLISHED AND ABSOLUTE...
...AND BECAUSE I DESIRE TO SEE YOU DANCE ONE FINAL, CLUMSY, DESPERATE WALTZ.
HA HA HA HA
THEN... KILL ME NOW... IF YOU CAN...
I WILL NOT... DANCE... FOR YOU...
I HAVE ABIGAIL.
AND THE RETURNED MAN LAUGHS...

...AND IN HOUMA A YOUNG SAILOR ON SHORELEAVE ASKS SALLY PARKS TO EXCUSE HIM, IT'S JUST THAT HE KNOWS HER FACE FROM SOMEWHERE...
...AND OUTSIDE LAFAYETTE, JODY HERBERT SUDDENLY DECIDES TO TAKE A RIDE ON UP TO THE BAYOU...
LA 311
...AND GUS PRITCHETT GAZES OUT OVER A SCHOOL-YARD ABANDONED TO SHADOW AND THINKS HOW SWELL IT IS TO BE BACK...
...AND IN MONROE, HATTIE DUPLANTIS SHUDDERS AND RESOLVES TO GO FOR A WALK RATHER THAN THINK ABOUT THE MESS IN THE BEDROOM...
...AND MARK NEWELL HAS FOUND A CAR...
HONK! ONK! ONK!
BIJOU
GMJ
PROUD TO BE COONASS
... AND EVERYTHING BAD WITHIN TWO HUNDRED MILES FINDS ITSELF HEADING FOR LOUISIANA WITHOUT KNOWING WHY...

...AND THE RETURNED MAN WALKS HOME, TO PREPARE FOR HIS MANY VISITORS.

CRAK!
KRIK
KRIK
KREEK
EEEK
CREEEEEEEIK!

HOW... LONG...?
HA HA HA HA HA HA HA HA HA HA
HOW LONG HAS SHE BEEN DEAD??
HA HA HA HA
HA HA HA HA HA HA HA!
NEXT: THE BRIMSTONE BALLET

SOPHISTICATED SUSPENSE
DC
75¢
31
DEC. 84
SWAMP THING

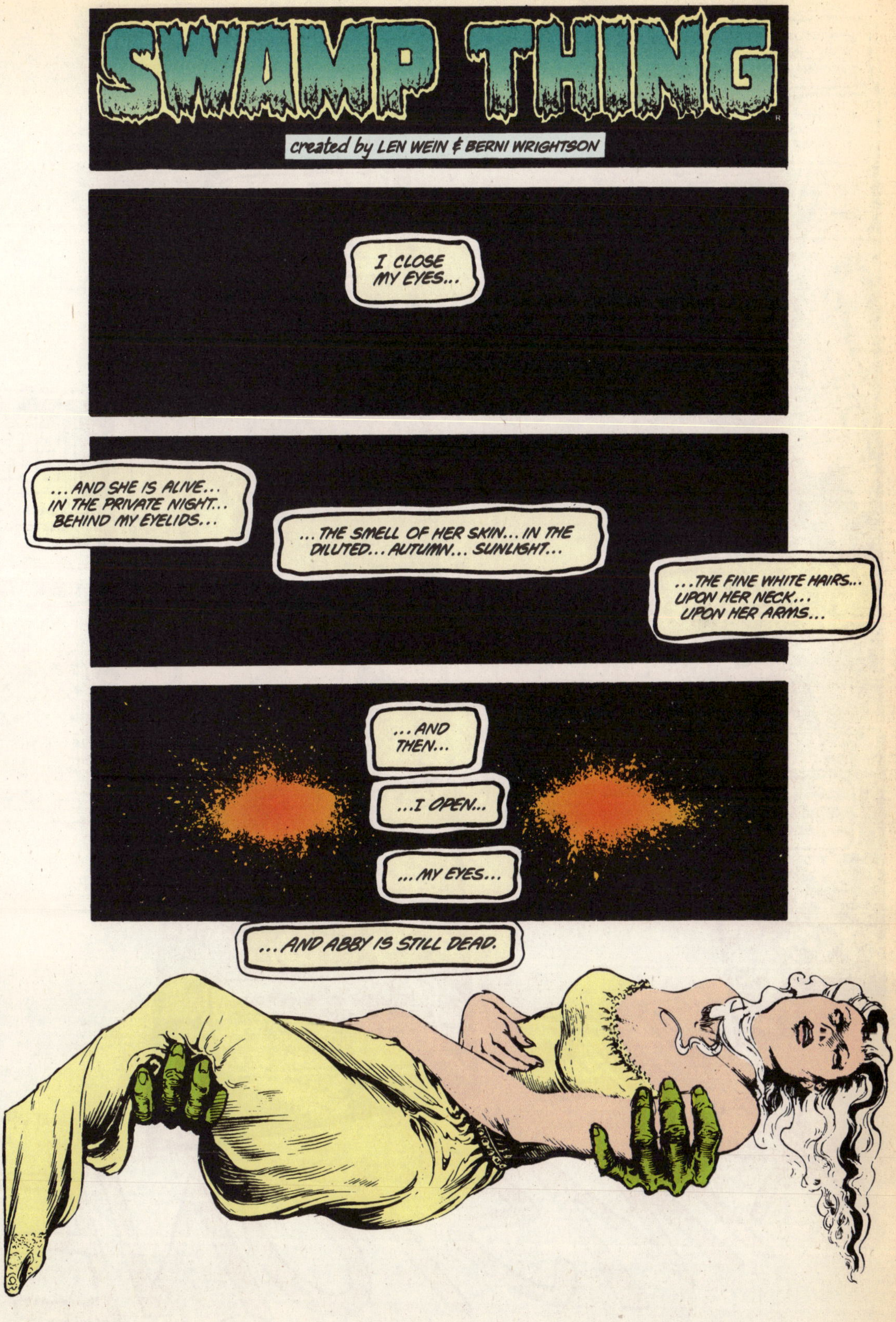
SWAMP THING
created by LEN WEIN & BERNI WRIGHTSON
I CLOSE MY EYES...
...AND SHE IS ALIVE... IN THE PRIVATE NIGHT... BEHIND MY EYELIDS...
...THE SMELL OF HER SKIN... IN THE DILUTED... AUTUMN... SUNLIGHT...
...THE FINE WHITE HAIRS... UPON HER NECK... UPON HER ARMS...
...AND THEN...
...I OPEN...
...MY EYES...
...AND ABBY IS STILL DEAD.

BEHIND ME... THE LAUGHTER OF MY ENEMY..., RATTLING IN ANOTHER MAN'S THROAT...
HIS CREATURES SWARM ABOUT US... COAGULATING... FROM THE TAINTED AIR...
HIS PRESENCE... CORRUPTS ITS TIMBERS...
THE WALLS... ARE SODDEN... WITH HIS VILENESS...
TO THINK... I MOURNED HIM ONCE WHEN HE WAS DEAD...
SHE MUST NOT REMAIN IN THIS PLACE.
"ONE FINAL, CLUMSY, DESPERATE WALTZ"... THAT IS WHAT HE PROMISED ME...
I STUMBLE THROUGH HIS CROOKED HOUSE... HER COLD, STILL WEIGHT... CRUSHED TO MY BREAST...
BENEATH MY FINGERTIPS... THE BANISTER... BECOMES A RIB CAGE... RAW AND EXPOSED...
THE BRIMSTONE
an ALAN MOORE WRITER * RICK VEITCH and JOHN TOTLEBEN ARTISTS * KAREN BERGER EDITOR *

SHE MUST NOT...
...REMAIN...
...IN THIS PLACE.
NO MATTER HOW GROTESQUE...
...OUR QUADRILLE MAY BECOME...
BALLET
TATJANA WOOD COLORIST * JOHN COSTANZA LETTERER presentation

WELL, HOLLAND?
HAVE YOU AT LAST LEARNED DESPAIR?
YOU DID NOT... HAVE TO KILL HER... TO TEACH ME DESPAIR, ARCANE...
...BUT YOU HAVE GIVEN ME... A DEEPER UNDERSTANDING...
...OF ABOMINATION.

OH, DEAR.
DID SHE MEAN SO MUCH TO YOU?
NEVER FEAR. I HAVE SOME GOOD NEWS...
SHE ISN'T DEAD AT ALL.
IT WAS ALL A HOAX!
THAT BREATHLESS CARCASS THAT YOU CRADLE SO PROTECTIVELY ...THAT ISN'T HER!
THAT'S JUST A CONSTRUCT, FORMED WITH THE ABILITIES I STOLE FROM MATTHEW CABLE ALONG WITH HIS FLESH.
AREN'T YOU ANGRY AT THE WAY YOU WERE DECEIVED?
WHY DON'T YOU RIP THE CONSTRUCT'S HEAD OFF?
YOU KNOW ...AS A GESTURE OF DEFIANCE...
YOU LIE.
THIS IS ABBY.
SHE IS DEAD.
YES!
REALLY DEAD.

WAIT!
WHERE ARE YOU GOING?
YOU CAN'T JUST WALK AWAY, HOLLAND. YOU HAVEN'T HEARD THE BEST OF IT YET...
YOU SEE, SHE ISN'T JUST DEAD...
SHE'S DAMNED, HOLLAND.
DAMNED TO HELL.
I RIPPED HER SOUL FROM HER AND IT PULSED IN MY HANDS, MILK WHITE AND TRANSLUCENT...
... AND THEN I HURLED IT DOWN INTO THE DEEPEST SEWERS OF THE AFTERWORLD...
... JUST TO HEAR IT SCREAM.
SUCH IS MY POWER... THE POWER TO CONDEMN A STAINLESS INNOCENT TO THE PIT...
THE POWER TO RESURRECT THE GUILTY DEAD AND DRESS THEM IN WARM NEW PROTO-PLASM...

"YOU MURDERED ME, HOLLAND.. YOU AND KRIPTMANN AND PALE, COLD ABIGAIL, LAUNCHING ME UPON A FLESHLESS ODYSSEY THROUGH THE DISMAL WATERS BEYOND DEATH.
"DARK FLOTSAM BOBBED UPON THOSE TIDES...
"I BROUGHT SOME BACK WITH ME."
THEY ARE RETURNED.
THE CREAM OF THE GALLOWS. THE ARISTOCRACY OF HELL.
THEY ARE OUT THERE NOW, CELEBRATING THEIR NEW SKIN IN THE DARKNESS.
"SALLY PARKS, FLIRTING IN HOUMA, TWENTY-TWO YEARS AFTER A POLICE MARKSMAN MADE A SMALL HOLE IN HER FOREHEAD, A LARGER ONE AT THE BACK...
"AS PRETTY, AS CAPTIVATING, AS PSYCHOTIC AS EVER.
"AND GUS PRITCHETT, PLUMP AND FATHERLY, WHO SMOTHERED CHILDREN IN ABANDONED REFRIGERATORS AND WENT TO THE ELECTRIC CHAIR IN 1964...
THEY ARE RETURNED, AND THEY ARE BUT THE FIRST.
"AND BETTY MONTCLAIR, WHO KILLED HERSELF IN A GARAGE AFTER COMMITTING A CRIME THAT CANNOT EASILY BE PUT INTO WORDS...
"AND MARK NEWELL...
"...AND ERIC LOVEDAY..."
IT IS THE APOCALYPSE...

MY APOCALYPSE!!
RUN, HOLLAND!
RUN ENCUMBERED WITH YOUR STUPID, POINTLESS BURDEN...
FOR THERE IS NO ROCK TO HIDE YOU...
NO BEACON OF INCORRUPTIBLE GOODNESS TO LIGHT YOUR WAY...

"NO CELESTIAL FORCE THAT WATCHES OVER US."
MONITOR? WHAT'S HAPPENING IN LOUISIANA?
THE SCREENS ARE GOING CRAZY...
MONITOR? I SAID...
I HEARD WHAT YOU SAID. PLEASE DO NOT DISTURB ME. I AM CONCENTRATING...
I AM ATTEMPTING TO SUPPRESS FOR THE FIRST TIME IN MY LIFE...
...THE UNCONTROLLABLE URGE TO LOOK AWAY.

I MUST NOT... WEAKEN NOW...
I HAVE MADE... TOO MANY MISTAKES... ALREADY...
DREAMS THAT WENT UNQUESTIONED...
I SEE MY UNCLE OVER THERE, TALKING TO MY HUSBAND. THEY'RE INSEPARABLE INSECTS, YOU KNOW...
THE WARNINGS UNHEEDED...
...YOUR PARENTS FREED THE MONKEY WITH A CHARM SPELLED OUT IN RANDOM LETTERS ON A BOARD.
WAS THERE SOME FURTHER FIEND THAT NUDGED THEIR ARM?
THE ANSWER, MADAME, IS FOR YOU TO KNOW...
THE OMENS IGNORED.
THIS IS THE FINAL BATTLE.
I MUST NOT WEAKEN NOW...

AREN'T YOU TIRED, HOLLAND?
TIRED OF ALL THIS POINTLESS RUNNING?
THE SWAMPS WILL NOT PROTECT YOU...
FOR THIS IS MY WORLD NOW...
THESE ARE MY SWAMPS...
...TO DO WITH AS I PLEASE!
YOU SURVIVE AT MY INDULGENCE, HOLLAND.
AFTER ALL THESE YEARS, THE VICTORY IS MINE.
THERE IS NO POINT IN RUNNING.
THERE IS... NO NEED... FOR RUNNING.
NOT NOW...

DON'T BE RIDICULOUS, HOLLAND. WHAT ARE YOU *TALKING* ABOUT?
YOU...HAVE MADE... A *MISTAKE*... ARCANE.
THINGS...HAVE *CHANGED*...SINCE YOU...WERE DEAD.
I...AM NOT... *HOLLAND*.
I AM... *SWAMP THING*.
I AM OF... THE *CLEAN EARTH*.
I AM IN... MY PLACE... OF *POWER*...
...AND YOU SHOULD NOT HAVE *COME* HERE!

YOU...
YOU HURT ME.
BUT... YOU HAVE NO MAGIC!
UNLESS...
SOME ELEMENTAL FORCE? BUT... WHEN I ENCOUNTERED YOU BEFORE, YOU...
NO, ARCANE...
YOU... HAVE NEVER... ENCOUNTERED... ME BEFORE.
THIS... IS OUR... FIRST BATTLE...

THIS... IS OUR... *FINAL*... *BATTLE*...
YOU CLAIM... THE EARTH... FOR YOUR OWN... ARCANE...
YET YOU HAVE NOT... ONE *TENTH*... OF THE EARTH'S *POWER*...
YOU... MOCK... GOD!
YOU MAKE... THE WORLD... *WORTHLESS*... WITH YOUR *LIES!*
HOW...
...DARE...
...YOU??

...AND ON THEIR WAY TO LOUISIANA, THE DARK SOULS THAT HE HAD SUMMONED STOP IN THEIR TRACKS AND STARE, CONFUSED, INTO THE CHURNING WHITENESS...
...AND IN HOUMA, A SAILOR STARTS SCREAMING AND SALLY PARKS DOESN'T KNOW WHY...
...UNTIL BLOOD TRICKLES DOWN HER CHEEK, AND SHE LIFTS HER HAND TO INVESTIGATE...
...AND A MILE OUTSIDE TOWN THE PREMISES OF BLACKRIVER RECORPORATIONS BEGIN TO LIQUEFY AND MELT, RELEASING A STENCH LIKE SPOILED MEAT...
BLACKRIVER RECORPORATIONS
...AND DEEP WITHIN THE BORROWED FLESH OF THE RETURNED MAN...
...SOMETHING STIRS...
NO.

NO!
NOT YOU!
LEAVE ME ALONE! THIS FLESH IS MINE NOW...
GET OUT! GET OUT!!
WE MADE A BARGAIN...
NO! YOU STOLE IT FROM ME... AND THEN YOU KILLED ABBY...
YOU WERE TOO STRONG FOR ME TO CHALLENGE BEFORE, BUT NOW...
MATT?
CABLE! THE POWER IS WANING! PLEASE...
GOOD... WE BOTH DESERVE IT...
JUST AS LONG... AS I GET TO SEND YOU...
...WHERE YOU SENT MY WIFE.
REMEMBER THE CAR CRASH? IT'S ONLY THE POWER THAT KEEPS THIS BODY ALIVE!
CABLE, YOU FOOL, YOU'LL KILL US BOTH.
GOOD-BYE, ARCANE.

I CLOSE MY EYES...
I LOOK AWAY...
BEHIND MY EYELIDS... IN THE PRIVATE NIGHT... I HEAR... THE SCREAM ... OF MY ENEMY...
NOOOOOOOOOOOOOOOOOOOOOOOOOOOOOOO
HE IS FALLING...
HIS UNCLEAN SPIRIT... TOO TORN... TOO BATTERED TO RESIST... THAT TERRIBLE GRAVITY...
AND IN HIS EYES... THE DREADFUL KNOWLEDGE...
...THE KNOWLEDGE... OF WHAT WAITS FOR HIM...
...BELOW...
AND THEN... HE HAS GONE...
...AND THERE IS ONLY...
...MATT?

HELLO... ALEC...
ARCANE... HAS GONE?
...BUT YOU... YOU ARE HURT...
...THESE WOUNDS THAT OPEN...
I'M DYING.
IT'S FOR THE BEST... AFTER WHAT I LET HIM DO...
MATT... HE POSSESSED YOU... HIS WAS THE ONLY EVIL...
NO.
NO. I LET HIM. I WAS WEAK...
THERE ISN'T ANY EVIL, ALEC... NO SPECIAL BLACKNESS RESERVED FOR DEMONS AND MONSTERS. THERE'S JUST WEAKNESS... I HAD A CHOICE...
MATT... YOU ARE RAMBLING...
YOUR POWER...
CAN'T YOU... REPAIR YOURSELF?
PERHAPS... ENOUGH POWER... TO REPAIR ONE...
BUT I... DON'T WANT TO... LIVE...
...AND IT ISN'T ME... THAT NEEDS... REPAIRING...

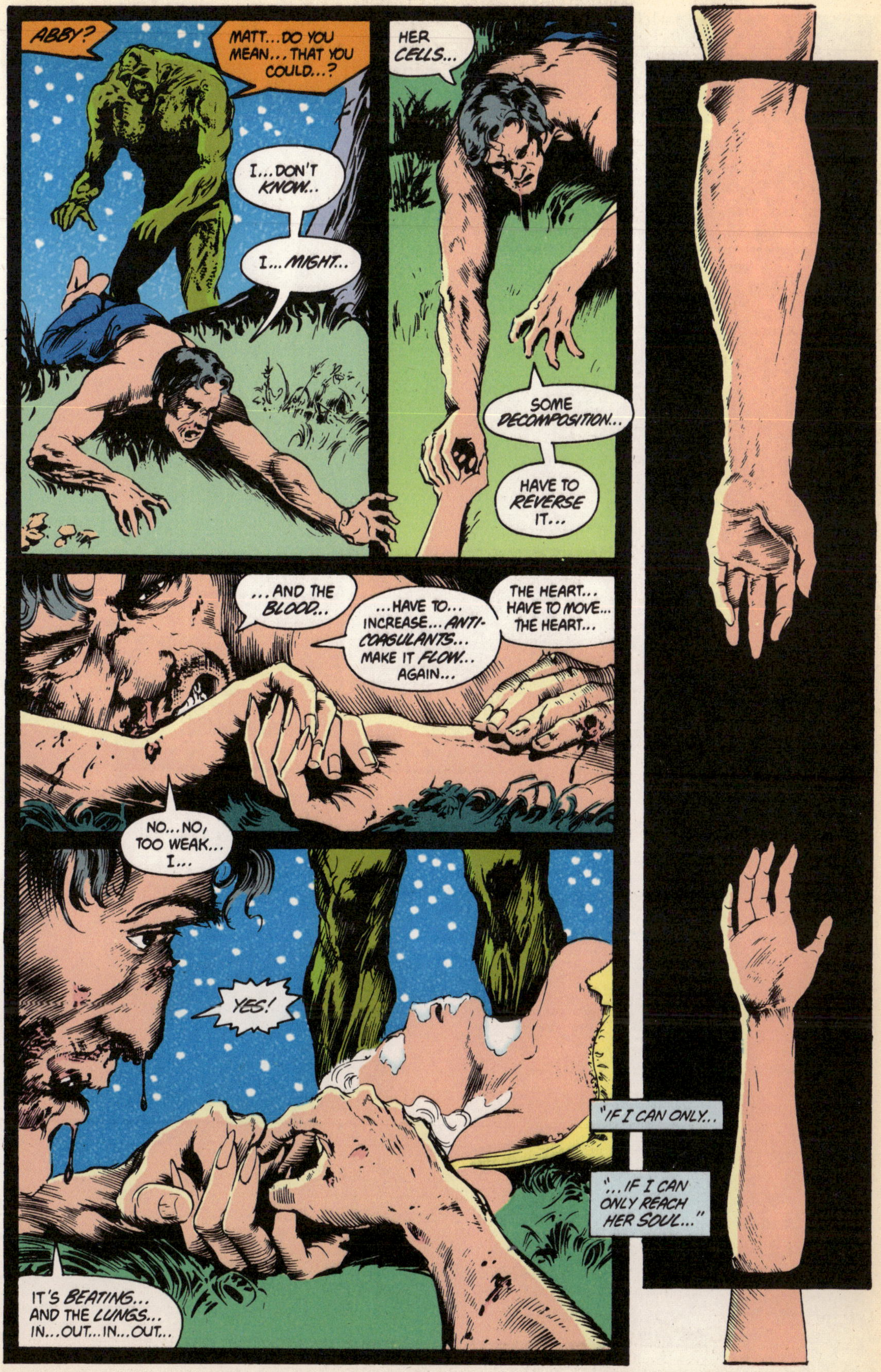
ABBY?
MATT...DO YOU MEAN... THAT YOU COULD...?
I...DON'T KNOW...
I...MIGHT...
HER CELLS...
SOME DECOMPOSITION...
HAVE TO REVERSE IT...
...AND THE BLOOD...
...HAVE TO... INCREASE... ANTI-COAGULANTS... MAKE IT FLOW... AGAIN...
THE HEART... HAVE TO MOVE... THE HEART...
NO...NO, TOO WEAK... I...
YES!
IT'S BEATING... AND THE LUNGS... IN...OUT...IN...OUT...
"IF I CAN ONLY...
"...IF I CAN ONLY REACH HER SOUL..."

I...
I'M SORRY, ALEC...
I'M...SO VERY...
...VERY... SOR

HOUMA 4 MILES
LOUISIANA STATE POLICE
WHAT A NIGHT! YOU REMEMBER A NIGHT LIKE THIS, BOBBY?
NO, I DON'T REMEMBER A NIGHT LIKE THIS.
ME NEITHER.
THOUGHT WE WAS NEVER GONNA GET THAT SAILOR IN THE DRUNK TANK...
ALL THAT STUFF ABOUT WOMEN WITH HOLES IN THEIR HEADS.
A FRUITCAKE.
YEAH, BUT WHAT ABOUT ALL THOSE PEOPLE TEDDY 'N' EARL PICKED UP ON THE INTERSTATE?
LITTLE KIDDIES WALKIN' ABOUT IN THE SNOW...
JEEZ!
WHAT IS IT, BOBBY?
WHY 'DYA PULL OVER? IS IT...?
OH.
LORDY!
THIS GUY'S BEEN IN SOME KINDA ACCIDENT ALL RIGHT. HE AIN'T HARDLY BREATHIN.' GOT STEERIN' COLUMN FRACTURES, THE WORKS...
LOOKS THAT WAY. BUT... UH...
...WHERE'S HIS CAR?

NIGHT LIKE THIS, WHO GIVES A DAMN?
C'MON... LET'S GET HIM IN OUR CAR. MAYBE WE CAN GET HIM TO THE HOSPITAL IN TIME...
YEAH. JEEZ, LOOK AT ALL THIS BLOOD..
I ONLY JUST GOT THROUGH CLEANIN' IT UP AFTER THE SAILOR...
KLIK
VROOOoooOMMMMM
SHE LIES... WHERE I LEFT HER...
SHE BREATHES... HER HEART BEATS...
BUT A HEARTBEAT... IS NOT A WOMAN... A BREATH... IS NOT ABBY...
HER BREAST MOVES...
...BUT IT IS EMPTY.
THERE IS... NO ONE THERE.
THE TEARS COME...
I CLOSE MY EYES...

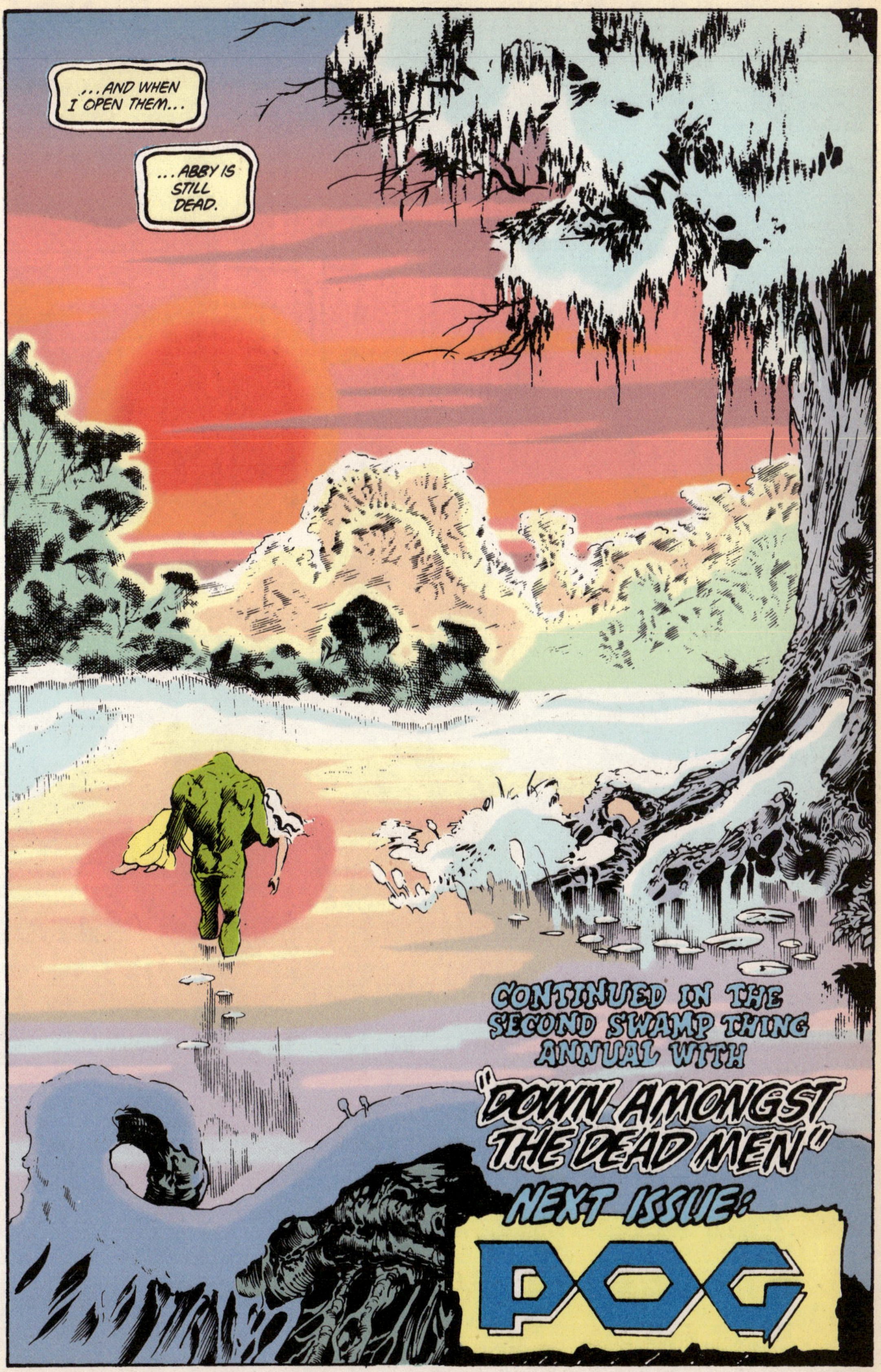
...AND WHEN I OPEN THEM...
...ABBY IS STILL DEAD.
CONTINUED IN THE SECOND SWAMP THING ANNUAL WITH
"DOWN AMONGST THE DEAD MEN"
NEXT ISSUE:
POG

DC
ANNUAL
1985
$1.25
CAN.$1.60
U.K. 45p
NO.2
SOPHISTICATED SUSPENSE
SWAMP THING
BY ALAN MOORE STEPHEN BISSETTE AND JOHN TOTLEBEN

THERE ARE PEOPLE.
THERE ARE STORIES.
THE PEOPLE THINK THEY SHAPE THE STORIES, BUT THE REVERSE IS OFTEN CLOSER TO THE TRUTH.
STORIES SHAPE THE WORLD. THEY EXIST INDEPENDENTLY OF PEOPLE, AND IN PLACES QUITE DEVOID OF MAN, THERE MAY YET BE MYTHOLOGIES.
THE GLACIERS HAVE THEIR LEGENDS. THE OCEAN BED ENTERTAINS ITS OWN ROMANCES.
EVEN HERE.
EVEN HERE, WITHIN THESE CHILL AND PERISHED THICKETS THAT KNOW NO WITNESS SAVE THE SLEEPING TOADS, EACH CURLED LIKE A GORGEOUS ALIEN FETUS BENEATH ITS STONE.
THERE ARE STORIES EVEN HERE.
STORIES THAT GROW, AS BLIGHTED TREES, INTO A TORMENTED PUZZLE. FRICTIONS THAT BECOME OVER-RIPE AND FESTER ON THE VINE.
THE STORIES HERE HAVE BLOSSOMED INTO DEFORMITIES, NURTURED BY A CURIOUS SOIL.
THERE ARE HEROES, THERE ARE WICKED UNCLES AND PRINCESSES, BUT THE DRAMA IS ASKEW. THE FAIRY TALE CONTORTS INTO A TRAGEDY...
THE HERO, SLOW AND MASSIVE, COMES TOO LATE...
THE WICKED UNCLE'S PASSING ACHIEVES NOTHING...
...AND THE PRINCESS FINDS NO CLICHÉ IN THE FATE THAT'S WORSE THAN DEATH.

CREATED BY
LEN WEIN & BERNI WRIGHTSON
SWAMP THING
DOWN AMONGST THE DEAD MEN
ALAN MOORE WRITER
STEVE BISSETTE & JOHN TOTLEBEN ARTISTS
KAREN BERGER EDITOR
TATJANA WOOD COLORIST
JOHN COSTANZA LETTERER

ABBY...
THIS BODY BREATHES...
ITS BLOOD MOVES...
IT DOES NOT DECAY...
...BUT WHERE ARE YOU?
HE SAID...THAT HE HAD RIPPED OUT...YOUR SOUL ...THAT HE HAD HURLED IT...RAW AND BLOODY... DOWN TO HELL.
ARCANE SAID THAT...
ARCANE SAID THAT... BEFORE HE DIED.
ABBY...
I WOULD FOLLOW YOU...
...I WOULD FOLLOW YOU EVEN THERE...
...BUT YOU... HAVE BEEN CAST INTO REGIONS... WHERE THE WEARING OF FLESH... IS PROSCRIBED...
...AND I... AM SHACKLED... TO THIS BODY.
NO I'M NOT.

ONCE BEFORE... I STEPPED OUTSIDE... THE CONFINES... OF THIS SHELL...
ONCE WHEN I WISHED TO ESCAPE... THE KNOWLEDGE... OF WHAT I WAS...
I CAN GO... BEYOND MY BODY...
...CAN I GO... BEYOND DEATH?
I REMEMBER...THAT THE FIRST STEP...WAS EASY...
NOT SO MUCH... AN EFFORT... AS A GREAT... RELAXATION...
I LAY DOWN...
I CLOSED MY EYES...
I LET GO... OF THE WORLD...
...AND SANK... BENEATH INFINITE... EMERALD FATHOMS.

ONCE MORE... I HEAR THE EARTH-PULSE... ITS TIMELESS, GEOLOGIC RHYTHM...
AGAIN I KNOW... THE CALL...OF THE PLANTWORLD... OF THE ROOTWEBS AND TREESPIRES...
...THE URGE...TO LET MY CONSCIOUSNESS... DISSIPATE...
TO DROWN... IN PEACE... AND SILENCE...
IT WOULD BE SO... EASY...
NO!
I MUST NOT... LOSE MYSELF... HERE.
MY GOAL IS... ELSEWHERE...
BEYOND THE GREEN...
BEYOND THE WORLD...
OF THE QUICK...
AND THE WARM...
BEYOND LIFE ITSELF.

CAN THIS... BE THE AFTERLIFE? CAN THIS BE... HEAVEN?
BUT WHY... IS IT... SO EMPTY? WAS THERE NO ONE... WHO WAS GOOD ENOUGH?
NO... NO, IT CANNOT BE... YET WHY... IS IT SO... DESERTED?
SO SILENT...?
OH MY GOD... HELLO? IS THAT SOMEBODY?
PLEASE, I NEED HELP... I GOT LOST IN THE FOG, AN' MY LITTLE BOY, HE'S AROUND HERE SOMEPLACE...
WHERE ARE WE? DO YOU WORK AROUND HERE?
LISTEN, YOU MUST THINK I'M CRAZY, BUT...
...BUT I KEEP TRYIN' TO REMEMBER HOW I GOT HERE, AN' I JUST CAN'T. I...
...I WAS DRIVING JERRY TO SCHOOL, AND...
I REMEMBER, JERRY WAS MAKIN' A NOISE IN THE BACK, SINGIN' THIS SONG FROM KIDDIE T.V. I TURNED AROUND TO SHUT HIM UP...
I WAS JUST PULLIN' OUT INTO THE INTERSECTION, AND...
...AND...
H-HEY...
HEY, WHERE AM I?
WUH-WHERE'S JERRY?

OH GOD...
OH GOD, THIS IS A NIGHTMARE!
PLEASE... PLEASE, I WANNA WAKE UP. I WANNA WAKE UP NOW!
MOM?
HEY, MOM, IT'S OKAY...
J-JERRY? WHERE...?
I'M SORRY, MOM. I COULDN'T FOLLOW, NOT RIGHT AWAY. BUT I'M HERE NOW ... WE CAN GO WHERE WE'RE SUPPOSED TO GO.
THANKS FOR LOOKING AFTER HER, MISTER.
JERRY... DO YOU KNOW THIS PLACE?
OH, SURE... IT'S NOT BEEN SO LONG SINCE I WAS HERE LAST TIME.
COME ON... THERE'S LIGHTS UP AHEAD...
WAIT!
COME BACK!
WHERE IS THIS PLACE?
BUDDY, IF ANYONE HERE HAD BREATH, I'D ADVISE YOU TO SAVE IT.
THEY WON'T BE COMING BACK.

INCIDENTALLY, NICE TO SEE YOU AGAIN, BIG FELLER.
PITY IT COULDN'T BE UNDER MORE PLEASANT CIRCUMSTANCES.
WHEN DID YOU DIE?
I... AM NOT... DEAD.
I AM HERE... OF MY OWN WILL...
WHO... ARE YOU? I DO NOT... REMEMBER YOU...
YOU WOULDN'T. IN YOUR WORLD I'M INVISIBLE. I'VE RUN INTO YOU ONCE OR TWICE, THOUGH.
THE NAME'S DEADMAN...
...AND IF YOU'RE STILL ALIVE, WHAT ARE YOU DOING IN THE REGION OF THE JUST DEAD?
"JUST DEAD"?
SURE... LIKE THAT WOMAN AND HER SON...
I SAW HER LEAVE HER BODY AND WANDER AWAY FROM THAT CAR-WRECK ON THE INTER-SECTION...
...BUT THE KID LIVED FOR A COUPLE OF MINUTES. I HUNG ON TO WAIT FOR HIM.
YOU HAVEN'T ANSWERED MY QUESTION.

I AM LOOKING... FOR A FRIEND... A WOMAN...
SHE WAS CAST OUT... FROM HER BODY... UNJUSTLY...
SHE DOES NOT... DESERVE TO BE HERE...
WHO DOES?
LISTEN... I ONLY RECENTLY DISCOVERED THIS ZONE MYSELF, BUT I'LL SHOW YOU AROUND THE BEST I CAN.
IF SHE'S HERE, WE'LL FIND HER.
THAT OKAY?
THANK YOU.
THIS PLACE... IT SHIFTS... CHANGES...
ECTOPLASM. THIS REGION IS CLOSEST TO THE LAND OF THE LIVING. AND ECTOPLASM IS A SORT OF SUB-MATTER THAT MIMICS THE FORMS OF THE REAL WORLD.
IF WE'RE LUCKY, WE MAY EVEN SEE...
AHH.
YEAH, I THOUGHT SO. OVER THERE...
POLTERGEISTS.
KEEP QUIET... THEY'RE GRAZING...

THEY'RE COMPLETELY MINDLESS. THEY JUST FORM FROM THE ECTO-FOG AT THE POINTS WHERE PARTICULARLY VIOLENT EMOTIONS SEEP THROUGH FROM THE LIVING WORLD.
IF YOU FLY THROUGH THEM, THEY BURST AND SMELL TERRIBLE.
HEH.
THERE ARE... FEW PEOPLE HERE...
RIGHT. WE GET A COUPLE WHO HANG AROUND, TOO SHOCKED TO REALIZE WHAT'S HAPPENED, BUT MOST FOLK MOVE ON WHEREVER THEY'RE GOING PRETTY QUICKLY.
WHEN DID YOUR FRIEND PASS THROUGH?
YESTERDAY.
HMMM...
IF SHE HADN'T GONE ON, I'D HAVE RUN ACROSS HER BY NOW. MAYBE WE SHOULD HEAD ON OVER TO THE LIGHTS. SHE MAY HAVE GONE THAT WAY...
... AND, FRANKLY, IF SHE'S GONE ANY OTHER WAY, YOU BETTER FORGET ABOUT HER.
THE LIGHTS? WHAT...
... LIGHTS?

THOSE LIGHTS.
UH, LISTEN... I'M NOT SUPPOSED TO GO BEYOND THIS POINT. FROM HERE ON YOU'LL HAVE TO GO IT ALONE.
I CAN WAIT HERE TILL YOU GET BACK...
ALONE?
GO ALONE... INTO... THE PRESENCE...
...OF GOD?
GOD?
THERE'S NO NEED TO WORRY. SHE ALWAYS TREATED ME OKAY...
SHE?
WELL...YEAH.
UH, LOOK, I DON'T KNOW WHAT YOU'RE EXPECTING, BUT AS I UNDERSTAND IT, THERE'S A WOMAN RUNNING THE SHOW. HER NAME'S RAMA KUSHNA...
AS FOR FINDING YOUR WAY AROUND, DO YOU KNOW ANYBODY HERE? MAYBE YOU COULD FIND SOME FRIENDS...
HE'LL FIND FRIENDS, BOSTON BRAND...
FRIENDS...
...AND OTHER STRANGERS.

OH.
IT'S YOU.
Y'KNOW, BEING *DEAD*, IT'S LIKE WAITING FOR A *BUS*...
YOU DON'T SEE ANYONE FOR MONTHS AND THEN TWO OR THREE ARRIVE TOGETHER...
COINCIDENCE IS THE SECRET THREAD THAT KNOTS THE WORLD *TOGETHER*, BOSTON BRAND. HAVE YOU BEEN DEAD THESE LONG YEARS WITHOUT LEARNING *THAT*?
THE STRANGER COMES WHERE THE STRANGER IS *REQUIRED*.
YEAH? REQUIRED BY *WHO*?
OKAY, "*I LOVE A MYSTERY*," PLAY IT YOUR WAY...
DEADMAN... I WILL BE... IN GOOD HANDS... WITH THE STRANGER. WE HAVE MET... BEFORE.
THANK YOU... FOR YOUR *HELP*.
PERHAPS... *ONE* DAY... I MAY HELP... *YOU*.
I SHOULD LIVE SO LONG.
ROTSA RUCK, KEED. I'LL SEE YOU AROUND...

STRANGER... I SEEK... A WOMAN...
YES. ABIGAIL CABLE...
ALTHOUGH HER EVENTUAL FATE IS UNKNOWN TO ME, I HEARD A LITTLE OF THE CONFLICT IN WHICH SHE WAS DISPLACED.
HER UNCLE, THE DEFEATED ANTON ARCANE, PLUNGED THROUGH THIS REGION ON HIS WAY TO HELL, A BLACK AND SHRIEKING COMET, SPITTING MOLTEN TAR...
THE NOISE AND THE STENCH WERE UNBEARABLE.
I KNEW THEN THAT THE LAST OF THE MATTER HAD NOT BEEN HEARD.
COME. IF WE ARE TO FIND YOUR FRIEND, WE MUST HURRY...
... ALTHOUGH, IN TRUTH, IT IS NOT VERY FAR.
THESE LIGHTS... I FEEL... AS IF I... REMEMBER THEM...
AS IF... I SAW THEM... ONCE... A LONG... TIME AGO...
YES. EVERYONE SAYS THAT.
NOW, HOLD MY HAND. WE'RE ALMOST...
... THERE.

THIS...IS HEAVEN?
IT IS AN ASPECT OF HEAVEN. HEAVEN HAS AS MANY SEMBLANCES AS THERE ARE CREEDS...
...AS THERE ARE SOULS.
YOU... KNOW IT... WELL?
IS... THIS... YOUR HOME?
MY HOME?
NO.
I FEAR I HAVE LONG SINCE BECOME A STRANGER IN PARADISE.

I DIDN'T THINK THERE WERE ANY STRANGERS IN PARADISE...
...IT'S FAR TOO SMALL FOR THAT.
ALEC?
ALEC... HOLLAND?
HOLLAND? THEN I FEAR I AM CONFUSED. I HAD BELIEVED THAT YOU WERE...
...ALEC HOLLAND.
YES... SO... DID I...
I'M GLAD YOU FOUND OUT EVENTUALLY...
...AND I OUGHT TO THANK YOU FOR HELPING ME GET HERE.
IT WAS... NOTHING...
ONLY... A BURIAL...
IT FREED ME. I'D BECOME OBSESSED WITH NOT LEAVING MY BODY THERE IN THE SWAMP.
AS A RESULT, I GOT STUCK BETWEEN EARTH AND THE REALM OF THE JUST-DEAD.
IT HAPPENS, SOMETIMES, WITH A VIOLENT DEATH...
...AND IF YOU ARE INDEED THE SHADE OF ALEC HOLLAND, THEN YOUR DEMISE WAS VIOLENT IN THE EXTREME.

YES.
THAT'S WHY I'M NOT ANXIOUS TO TAKE UP THE OPTION TO REINCARNATE FOR A WHILE, EVEN THOUGH LINDA WANTS TO...
LINDA? SHE IS HERE?
WHERE ELSE?
SHE WANTS TO GO BACK ON THE MERRY-GO-ROUND, HAVE SOME CHILDREN. YOUR WORLD WILL NEED CHILDREN SOON...
WHY DID YOU COME HERE? YOU'RE NOT DEAD...
I... AM LOOKING... FOR ABIGAIL... CABLE...
IN YOUR LIFETIME... YOU DID NOT... KNOW HER...
SHE MAY... HAVE PASSED... THIS WAY...
I KNOW THE WOMAN YOU MEAN. SHE HASN'T BEEN BY HERE, OR I'D HAVE SEEN HER.
LIKE I SAID, IT'S A SMALL PLACE...
ALEC?
COMING, SWEETHEART...
LISTEN, WHY NOT COME AND SAY HELLO TO LINDA? I'VE TOLD HER ABOUT YOU...
NO.
NO... I DON'T THINK SO... WE...
WE... HAVE... TO GO NOW... THANK YOU... FOR YOUR HELP...
ANY TIME.

SHE... WAS NOT THERE.
NO.
I FEAR WE HAVE BUT ONE PLACE LEFT TO TRY.
YES...
I... I HAD... HOPED... THAT ARCANE... LIED...
STRANGER...? IT GROWS... COLD...
INDEED... AND COLDER STILL WITH EACH STEP WE TAKE FROM HIS MYSTERIOUS PRESENCE...
FROM HIS ETHEREAL CONTINENT OF PERPETUAL AFTERNOON.
"HIS"?
BUT... DEADMAN SAID... THAT GOD... WAS *FEMALE*...
BOSTON BRAND IS A YOUNG SPIRIT. HE HAS SEEN BUT A FEW JIGSAW FRAGMENTS...
...OF A DESIGN THAT SPREADS OUTWARD FOREVER.
NOW COME...
LET US SEEK *PERMISSION* FOR OUR DESCENT TO *PANDEMONIUM*.

PERMISSION...?
OF COURSE. THE ORDERED UNIVERSE IS BUT A MICROSCOPIC BUBBLE IN AN OCEAN OF SEETHING MADNESS.
THE FORCES BEYOND THIS POINT ARE NOT TO BE LIGHTLY DISTURBED...
THUS, THERE IS ONE WHO IS APPOINTED TO THIS DISMAL TERRITORY AS A SENTINEL, THOUGH OFTEN HIS DUTIES TAKE HIM ELSEWHERE.
HE IS HERE NOW.
BUT... THERE IS... NOTHING...
NOTHING BUT... BLACKNESS...
THE BLACKNESS IS A PART OF WHAT HE IS. NOW PREPARE YOURSELF...
...AS HE REVEALS THE LIGHT.
THAT BAND... OF WHITENESS... GROWING WIDER...
STRANGER...?
WHAT IS... HAPPENING?
HAPPENING?
CAN'T YOU GUESS?

HE'S OPENING HIS EYES.

WHO APPROACHES... THE SPECTRE?
ARE YOU NATIVE TO THESE BORDERLANDS OF FORM AND REASON?
NO.
A STRANGER.
AHH.
IT IS YOU, BROTHERLESS ONE...
...AND ANOTHER BESIDE YOU? I SHALL CONDENSE MY SUBSTANCE THAT I MAY SEE HIM MORE KEENLY.
TTHERE THERE THERE THERE THERE
THERE.
AN EARTH ELEMENTAL.
HOW STRANGE. I HAD THOUGHT THEM ALL LONG SINCE DESTROYED...
WHAT IS YOUR NAME, CREATURE, AND WHY HAS THE GRAY WALKER BROUGHT YOU TO ME?
I...
I... AM... THE SWAMP THING...
I SEEK... A FRIEND...

THERE ARE NO FRIENDS IN THIS PLACE.
IT IS TOO LARGE.
DO YOU REFER TO THE WOMAN ABIGAIL CABLE?
YOU...?
YOU...HAVE... SEEN HER?
OF COURSE.
SHE IS CONSIGNED TO THE UNSPEAKABLE REALMS BENEATH...
...AND THAT IS WHERE SHE MUST STAY!
STAY...?
NNNNOOOOOOO!!
CONTAIN YOURSELF! THIS IS ONE WHO CANNOT BE FOUGHT.
SPECTRE! HEAR ME! THE WOMAN WAS CONDEMNED BY ONE WHO HAD NO RIGHT!

ALL THAT HAPPENS, HAPPENS BY DECREE OF ONE WILL.
THERE IS ONE VOICE THAT SPEAKS IN ALL THINGS.
IF THE WOMAN IS CONDEMNED, THEN THAT IS THE FATE SET ASIDE FOR HER.
BUT IF SHE IS UNJUSTLY CONDEMNED TO HELL, THEN HELL HAS NO REASON...
...AND IF THAT IS SO, SPECTRE, THEN PARADISE ITSELF IS AN EMPTY CONFECTION.
PERHAPS...
YET, IF THINGS ARE AS YOU SAY, THEN WOULD NOT HER RETURN FROM DEATH RENDER LIFE ITSELF MEANINGLESS?
SUCH THINGS ARE NOT ALLOWED, STRANGER.
NO?
THEN WHAT OF JIM CORRIGAN?
HAHAHAHAHAHA HAHA HAHAHAHAHA HA!!
YOUR CLEVERNESS HAS NOT DIMMED, STRANGER, NOR YOUR IMPUDENCE.
OF ALL THE PRESENCES, YOU WERE ALWAYS MY FAVORITE.
YOU MAY PASS.

STRANGER...
WHO WAS... JIM CORRIGAN...?
HE WAS...
...WHILE HE LIVED.

THIS PLACE...
IT IS... *TERRIBLE...*
NOT SO TERRIBLE AS OUR *DESTINATION.*
WE ARE APPROACHING THE VERY *EDGE* OF RATIONAL BEING HERE.
WHAT YOU SEE ABOUT YOU IS BUT THE *THUMB-PRINT* OF *CHAOS.*
A LITTLE WAY AHEAD THE SENSELESS RAGING OF THE *CHAOPLASM* BEGINS, AND CONTINUES OUT TO *INFINITY.*
WE APPROACH THE LAST PLACE THAT CAN TRULY BE *CALLED* A PLACE.
AND... THIS *PLACE...*
IT IS... *HELL?*

OH YES.
THE GATES WILL OPEN AS YOU APPROACH. I CANNOT ACCOMPANY YOU BEYOND THIS POINT. EACH SOUL MUST ENTER *ALONE*...
... OTHERWISE, HOW COULD IT TRULY BE *HELL*?
WITHIN THIS PLACE ARE CREATURES THAT WOULD TEAR THE WINGS FROM *ANGELS* AS A MOMENT'S RESPITE FROM BOREDOM.
ANSWER ME ONLY ONCE: DO YOU WISH TO *CONTINUE*?
I DO.

AHH...
IT WARMS MY HEART TO MEET WITH THEE AGAIN...
...AND MEET WITH COURAGE, FREE FROM HESITATION...
...OR CAN IT BE YOU ARE NAME OF PAIN...
...AND SIMPLY LACKING IN IMAGINATION?
NO MATTER. I AM CONFIDENT YOUR PLAN AFFORDS AMUSEMENT RARE...
...FOR ETRIGAN.

ETRIGAN.
AH, YES. THE DEMON THAT FANCIES HIMSELF HALF A MAN.
I HAVE HEARD OF YOU.
"OH, KETTLE! THOU ART BLACK!" THE POT EXCLAIMS. I KNOW ONE MORE AMBIVALENT FAR THAN I...
A LONELY SOUL, WHO, MENTIONING NO NAMES, WILL NOT CHOOSE 'TWIXT THE SULFUR AND THE SKY.
WHO WILL NOT SERVE ABOVE, NOR REIGN BELOW, BUT WALKS A PATH 'TWEEN MOLOCH AND THE MANGER.
WHO DO I SPEAK OF? IS IT ONE WE KNOW? OR COULD I BE REFERRING TO...
ENOUGH.
YOUR DISTORTIONS, THOUGH CUNNINGLY EXPRESSED, FAIL TO ENTERTAIN ME.
I DO NOT WISH TO HEAR ANY MORE OF THIS.
IF YOU HAVE COME TO MOCK, THEN BEGONE TO WHATEVER PIT SPAWNED YOU.
TO MOCK? WHAT? I? 'TIS HELP, SIR, THAT I BRING...
...JUST AS THE BRUTE BESIDE YOU AIDED ME WHEN I PURSUED THE DREADFUL MONKEY KING.
I WOULD REPAY HIS KINDNESS...
...FOR A FEE.
A FEE?
AND WHAT IS THE PRICE OF A DEMON'S HIRE?
YOU MAY DECIDE. WHATEVER SUITS YOU BEST.
WHAT IS THIS BLOOM YOU WEAR UPON YOUR BREAST?

THIS?
IT IS A FLOWER, PLUCKED UPON THE WESTERN SLOPE OF HEAVEN.
HOW PRECIOUS. LET THIS BLOSSOM BE MY FEE, TO PLANT WITHIN YON DARK SATANIC MILL...
...AND HAVE ITS BEAUTY THERE FOR ALL TO SEE, COMPARED WITH WHICH, HELL SHALL GROW BLEAKER STILL.
NOW, GATHER TO ME, CREATURE OF THE FEN, AND WE SHALL WALK, AS ONE, BEYOND THOSE WALLS 'MIDST SHRIEKING MAIDS AND SOBBING GENTLEMEN.
THE GATES SWING OPEN! THE INFERNO CALLS!
ETRIGAN! WAIT!
YOU CANNOT ACCOMPANY HIM! THE RULES...
THE RULES? AND IF I BREAK THESE RULES, PRAY TELL SHALL I BE PUNISHED?
SENT, PERHAPS, TO HELL?
HAHAHAHAHAHAHA
HAHAHAHAHAHAHAHA
HA HA HA!

ETRIGAN... THE ONE I SEEK...
HAVE YOU... SEEN...HER?
HOW COULD I MISS HER, IN THIS FORTRESS DIRE, WHERE ALL ONCE WARM AND SWEET GROWS COLD AND SOUR?
AGAINST THE GRIME AND ROT AND BLOOD-STREAKED MIRE SHE STOOD...
...AS PALE, AS RADIANT...
...AS A FLOWER.
HO! ETRIGAN PLANTS FLOWERS!
WE'D HEARD THAT YOU WERE NOW HALF A MAN...
...BUT IT SEEMS THAT YOU ARE RATHER HALF A WOMAN!
MUTTLECRAUNCH, YOU TUMOROUS EXCRESCENCE, HAVE A CARE! ETRIGAN'S A RHYMING DEMON NOW, AND FAR ABOVE SUCH BANTER WITH HIS KIN.
AREN'T YOU, ETRIGAN?
FRIENDS MUTTLECRAUNCH AND FLUTCH, YOUR WIT REMAINS LESS CAUSTIC THAN THE POX WHICH GNAWS YOUR BRAINS.
TO SPARE YOUR THROATS, RESPOND WITHOUT DELAY: WE SEEK A WOMAN. HAS SHE PASSED THIS WAY?

A WOMAN? PERHAPS MY SERVANT MAY HAVE NOTICED...
SERVANT?
WHAT, PRAY TELL, ARE YOU DOING?
P-POLISHING YOUR HOOVES, LORD MUTTLECRAUNCH. YOU SAID...
WITH A RAG? YOU WIPE THE FILTH FROM MUTTLECRAUNCH'S HOOVES WITH A RAG??
WHAT DO YOU THINK WE LET YOUR TONGUE GROW BACK FOR??
I THINK I'LL TEAR IT OUT AGAIN, TO REFRESH YOUR MEMORY...
OH NO. PLEASE DON'T. NOT AGAIN...
SUNDERLAND?
HOLLAND?
THE SWAMP CREATURE?
YOU!
IT WAS YOU WHO SENT ME HERE! YOU DID THIS TO ME...
BE STILL, MY LITTLE SLUG-PUDDINGS. WE CAN'T HAVE YOU OFFENDING LORD ETRIGAN'S GUEST!
NMMF
WHY, HE MIGHT READ US SOME MORE OF HIS POEMS! NUH HUH HUH HUH...
LET US DEPART. THEIR WORTHLESSNESS IS CLEAR.
WE SHALL NOT FIND THE FLOWER OF HADES HERE.

DEMON...
HOW... COULD GOD... ALLOW... SUCH A PLACE?
THINK YOU GOD BUILT THIS PLACE, WISHING MAN ILL AND NOT LUSTS UNCONTROLLED OR SWORDS UNSHEATHED?
NOT GOD, MY FRIEND. THE TRUTH'S MORE HIDEOUS STILL: THESE HALLS WERE CARVED BY MEN WHILE YET THEY BREATHED.
GOD IS NO PARENT OR POLICEMAN GRIM DISPENSING TREATS OR PUNISHMENTS TO ALL.
EACH SOUL CLIMBS OR DESCENDS BY ITS OWN WHIM. HE MOURNS, BUT HE CANNOT PREVENT THEIR FALL.
WE SUFFER AS WE CHOOSE. NOTHING'S AMISS. ALL TORMENTS ARE DESERVED...
...NONE MORE THAN THIS.
HUH-HOLLAND?
HUH-HOW NUH-NICE TO SEE YOU...

HELLO, ARCANE.
I MUH-MUST LOOK QUITE A MUH-MESS...
INSECT EGGS, YOU KNOW. HUH-HATCHING. INSUH-SIDE ME...
VERY APPROPRIATE. HA HA HA HA...
SUH-STILL, I HUH-HAD MY RUH-REVENGE, DIDN'T I? YUH-YOU HAVE CUH-COME FOR MUH-MY NIECE, I TAKE IT?
SHE'S UP AHEAD...
WUH-WHEN YOU SUH-SEE HER, YOU WON'T WUH-WANT HER...
NUH-NO! WAIT! PUH-PLEASE, BEFORE YOU GUH-GO...
HUH-HOW MANY YEARS HAVE I BUH-BEEN HERE?
SINCE YESTERDAY.
YESTERDAY?
EEEEEEEEEEEEEEEEE

HE SAID THAT... SHE WAS AHEAD... THAT I WOULD NOT WANT HER...
AHEAD? IN TRUTH, I'LL OWN SHE SEEMS TO BE. AS FOR HIS LAST ASSERTION...
...WE SHALL SEE.
ABBY?
THE HAIR WOULD MAKE A STYLISH FLY-WHISK, RUNDELTHRATT.
TAKE THE HAIR.
AND LEAVE THE EYES AS PENDANTS FOR SUCH WAX-ENCRUSTED EARS AS THINE, FESTLEQUIRM? FASTEN YOUR GOB, FELLOW...
NO!
GET...
AWAY...
FROM...
...HER.

ABBY...
OH, ABBY...
HE PUSHED US TO ONE SIDE, RUNDELTHRATT.
I NOTICED. WHAT SHOULD WE DO?
PEEL HIM AND SET HIM TO TASK IN THE SALT MINES, PERHAPS, OR...
YOU...
...HAVE DONE...
ENOUGH!!

THE BUGGER'S BLED MY NEB! IT IS SOME ELEMENTAL...
FOOL! WOULD YOU FIGHT ALL HELL? YOUR PRIZE IS WON! TAKE UP YOUR FALLEN BLOSSOM NOW, AND RUN!
SO, ETRIGAN HALF-A-MAN, YOU AND THE EARTH-GENII WORK TOGETHER TO DEPRIVE US OF OUR SPOILS!
I HAD HEARD YOU HAD GROWN SOFT WITH MORTALS.
WHAT BRIBE WERE YOU OFFERED?
I GAINED A FLOWER. HE TAKES ONE, IN RETURN. AS FOR MY SOFTNESS, JUDGE IT...
"...AS YOU BURN!"
HHAULPFSSHH!
THE HALF-A-MAN HAS TURNED UPON HIS KIN!
LET US RIP THE CONCEITED VERSES FROM HIS THROAT, ALONG WITH THE VEINS!

NO!
YOU RUH-RESCUED HER!
BUT THUH-THAT WAS MY REVENGE! THAT WAS ALL I HAD LUH-LEFT IN THIS PLACE! SHE MUST STUH-STAY!
DUH-DAMNED LIKE ME...
DAMNED LIKE MEEEEEEE
AS FLIES AROUND SPOILED MEAT THEY CONGREGATE, HOT FOR REVENGE, EACH SLOBBERING LIKE A HOUND...
IF SHE YOU CLASP IS TO AVOID THEIR FATE--
--WE MUST BE SWIFT TO GAIN THE HIGHER GROUND!
CLIMB! THOUGH I MAY REMOVE YOU FROM THIS PLACE, THE MAGICKS USED REQUIRE BOTH TIME...
...AND SPACE.

CLIMB FASTER, SCUM-FLAGONS! DON'T GIVE HIM PAUSE TO OPEN A CHYMIC WINDOW!
B-BUT, LORD RUNDELTHRATT... HE EMPLOYS THE EXHALATION INFERNAL...
CLIMB!
ETRIGAN... THEY ARE ALMOST... UPON US...
BE STILL! 'TIS SPACE ITSELF I SEEK TO REND.
ONE SLIP MAY TEAR THE CLOTH FROM END TO END!
THOU QUANTUM IMPS AND CHERUBS BY WHOSE DANCE IS SUBSTANCE FORMED TO SHAPE THE FIELDS, WE KNOW YOUR PERFECT WALTZ THAT CONJURES FORM FROM CHANCE MUST PAUSE, TO FREE US FROM THESE WASTES BELOW.
BY ROOT OF MINUS NINE AND CIRCLE SQUARED SET RIGHT AND TRUE AGAINST DIMENSIONS THREE LET OUR ILL-ANGLED PASSAGE BE PREPARED BETWEEN THE FOLDS...
...OF RARE GEOMETRY.
AAAAA!

THE PORTAL IS DILATED! KICK HIM FREE! YOU HAVE NO TIME TO WASTE ON SUCH AS HE!
ARCANE! LET GO...
I HATE YOUDIESCUMKILL YOU MURDER EATYOURBRAINS HATE TEAR YOUR HEARTKILLYOU DEADDEADDEAD
SKWNCH
UUK
NOW, TAKE HER FROM THESE STEWS AND FROZEN LAKES. SHE WILL REMEMBER NOT WHAT DID OCCUR, BUT IF IT PLEASE YOU, TELL HER WHEN SHE WAKES...
... A FLOWER GROWS YET IN HELL THAT'S NAMED FOR HER
HA HA HA HA HA HA HA HA HA HA HA HA HA HA HA HA HA HA HA

A-ALEC?
WH...?
OH, IT'S FREEZING! WHAT THE HELL ARE WE DOING OUT HERE IN THE SNOW?
UH, ALEC...? WHAT'S THE MATTER?

YOU'RE CRYING.
ALAN MOORE, SRBISSETTE & JTOTLEBEN 6-8/84

SOPHISTICATED SUSPENSE
75¢
32
JAN 85
SWAMP THING
BISSETTE & TOTLEBEN 8·23·84

FROM THE LOG OF THE VIVI-QUINQUEREME "FIND THE LADY":
"CERTAIN ENOUGH, OUR LANDING WAS MORE OR LESS A DISAPPOINTMENT.
"THE TADLING'S PORTAPUDDLE JUST ABOUT DECANTED AGAIN, AND THE JUNIOR UMBRELLA-BIRDS GOT WET HOLDING IT STEADY, OF WHICH THEY ARE FOREVER COMPLAINING.
"'FIND THE LADY' HELD UP CONSIDERABLE WELL TO THE ENTRY-BURN, SO IT APPEARS THAT DR. STRIGIFORME WAS WRONG ABOUT THAT... BUT THEN HE MOSTLY IS, THESE WHILES.
"MYSELF AND FRONT-MATE BARTLE FOUND OURSELVES OCCUPIED WRESTLING THE HYSTRICIDE INTO HIS DANGLEWEB, TO STOP HIM ROLLING AROUND PUNCTURING HIS SKIN.
"APLODONTIA USED TO HANDLE HIM SO EASY. I WISH SHE WAS STILL ALIVE.
"HE WAS RAVING FEARSOMELY BAD. JUST BEFORE US MAKING OUR FIRST BOUNCE, I HEARD HIM SHOUT 'THERE IS NO LADY!' AND THEN 'TRIFLES! TRIFLES LIGHT AS AIR!'
"I HOPE HE'S WRONG THIS TIME.
"I HOPE IT MOST VIGOROUSLY."
--POG. (SHIPBOSS) AE: 8491.4.01.

an ALAN MOORE . SHAWN McMANUS . KAREN BERGER . TATJANA WOOD . JOHN COSTANZA Presentation
WRITER ARTIST EDITOR COLORIST LETTERER

FNIF
MHHM.
ATMOSPHERICALS ABOUT TOLERABLE TO MIDDLING, AND GRAVITIES SUFFICIENT TO KEEP THE STUMP-WATER SETTING IN THE STUMP.
BY MY CALCULATEMENTS, YOU CAN DISENTRAIL WITH COMPLETE DIPLOMATIC IMPUNITY...
CHLIK
I... UH...

I... THINK WE FOUND THE LADY.
WE FOUND HER? AFTER ALL THESE INTERMINATIONS AND MILLENDERINGS? YOU'RE NOT ABMUSING ME, BOSS?
MAKING ABMUSEMENTS? ABOUT THE LADY? DEFINFINITELY NOT!
GO HELP DISTRANGLE THE HYSTRICIDE AND TELL THE UMBRELLABIRDS TO BREAK OUT THE SKIPS...
...AND DON'T BE UNMEMBERED TO TELL THE TADLING, AND SEE IF OLD STRIGIFORME IS FETCHABLE NOWABOUTS...
A NEW LADY! A NEW LADY AS ENVIRGINOMENTAL AS THE OLD ONE!
HUFF! SOUNDS LIKE AN INCOPROBULL DISLUSION TO ME.
THERE IS NO LADY, SAVE HER LONG SINCE ABANDONED TO THE LONELIEST ANIMALS OF ALL.
WE SEARCH AND ROOTLE 'MIDST THE NEBULAE, MERELY TO OCCUPY OUR TEDIOUS IMMORTALHOOD! WE...
WE...
UH...
HUMF.
I...
I AM OF A SUDDEN BECOME QUITE UNACCOUNTABLY LACHRYMOUS...

IT LOOKS LIKE HER. IT SMELLS LIKE HER...
OF COURSE, IT CANNOT ACTUALLY BE HER, NOT IN THIS REGRETERNAL MISERIVERSE, BUT...
BUT...
PESTIMISTIC OLD SOURQUILL! AS CO-CREATURE AND SHIPBOSS, I COMMASK YOU TO SHUSH YOUR CYANICISMS!
LET'S HOP A SKIP AND SEE IF THERE'S LOGICAL ANIMALATIONS HEREBY...
WITH RELIGHTED DELUCTANCE, I FOLLOW.
PSSHH! LUCCA YONDERWARDS...
UH...
HELLO, CUZLING.
IS THIS YOUR LADY WE'RE TREADLING ACROSS?

PERHAPS HE JUST FEELS UN-PARTIAL TO PROVERBALIZING RIGHT NOW...
HMM. IT'S HARD TO CONFIGURE THE ANGLES ON A FAUREIGNA, ESPECIALLY WHEN HE'S INVERTICALLY INCLINED.
OH, THEY'LL COME AROUNDWAYS AND SPLIT THE DIFFERACIAL. THEY JUST LIKE US, ONLY MORESO ANTISOCIABLE AND A MITE SMALLER...
...WHICH IS PECURIOUS, CONSITUATING THAT THEIR LADY IS SO BIG.
BIG ENOUGH FOR US TO REPOPLICATE AND RAISE OUR CELLU-LITTERS?
ENOUGH, AND ENOUGHER STILL!
JUST WISH THE OTHERS HAD SURVAILED LONG ENOUGH TO WATCH THEIR TUBE-TYKES SPROGGING UP...
STILL, LEASTWISE OLD "FIND THE LADY" WON'T BE OBLIGED TO SING THE EXTINCT-SONG NO MORE, NOW WE'RE HEREABOUTS...
THAT'S A MERCY AND A DELIVERATION. HE WAS STARTING TO UNMEMBER THE WORDS, AND...
WHUURP!
POG?
ARE YOU UNCONTUDED?
FORTUNATURALLY, I AM. I JUST SKITTLED OVER THIS HERE...
OVER THIS...

SWAMP THING
CREATED BY
LEN WEIN and BERNI WRIGHTSON

THAT UNTOLLIGIBLE GRUTTERING... CAN THAT BE A REAL LINGUISH?
WHO CARES? IT'S GOING TO SPLASTER US ALL OVER ITS SWOMPING GROUND!
GOOD BYE-AND-BYE, OLD POG...
EVERYBODY CLUTCH FOR THE CUMULATIONS AND REMAIN EMOTIONLESS!!
PRECARE FOR A DEMONSTRIFICATION, YOU SHUMBLING SCUMBOGGERY!
NO, STRIGIFORME! THAT SPOTGUN'S A RUSKERY GENTIQUE!
SEE?
WORKS SMOOTH AS A NEW-BOUGHT BABY-BEAKER'S BASE!

FETCH SOME *ANIMANACLES*, AND STAREFUL AS YOU *GO!* THERE'S PROSSIBLY *MORE* OF THESE *MUDSTERS* LOUCHING HEREAROUND!
YOU UNDISTRAUGHTED YET, BOSS?
I'M... I'M WELL AS CAN BE INSPECTED, BARTLE...
IT'S JUST... WHEN I SAW THAT SHAPERITION, I THOUGHT... I THOUGHT IT WAS...
...THE LONELIEST ANIMAL OF ALL?
YES.
...BUT I CAN SEE NOW IT ISN'T ANYMAL AT *ALL*. IT'S SOME SORT OF *AVEGINATION*...
THERE! THE FLORRIFYING MOSSTROSITY IS IMPINIONED! LET US RETINUE OUR *EXPLORI-GATIONS*...
OH, YOU TROTTLE ON AFOREWARDS.
I CONTEND TO JUST SET HEREWHILES.
WELL, IF YOU'RE SURE YOU'RE SETTLED IN COMPLETE LUXECURITY, WE'LL GO AND INQUEST AFTER SOME MORE *CUZLINGS*.
UH...
HELLO?

SEEMS I WAS UNCONFUTABLE IN MY QUESTIMATION. THAT IS SOME VARIETY OF LINGUISH YOU'RE DECLAMMERING.
YOU'RE AN INTELLICOMMUNICATING LIFE-FORM!
HMM. I DON'T MUCH CARE TO SEE A CO-CREATURE ENSTRAINED. SAW AN EXCESSANT SUM OF INDIQUITIES LIKE THAT BACK ON THE OLD LADY.
I'M GOING TO DISPOWER THE ANIMANACLES.
PLEASE DON'T DISCORPSIFY ME.
L-LIKEWISE.

I *KNEW* YOU WOULDN'T BE ANTAGRAVATED. YOU'RE MADE OUT OF THE SAME INGREENIENTS AS *THE LADY*.
YOU MUST BE HER *GUARDINER*, OR SOME SUCH.
I CONFIGURE *WE* MUST HAVE STARTLIZED *YOU* AS MUCH AS REVICE-VERSIONAL. I WISH I COULD *EXPLACATE*, BUT I DON'T SQUEAK YOUR LINGUISH, SO...
WHAT ARE YOU DROODLING?
SPIKTURES AND ANIMAGLYPHS? YOU THINK WE COULD COMMUNIFY IN *PICTOMIME*?
WELL, I GUESS THAT'S HOW WE FIRST MANAGED INTER-SPEECHES CONVERGATION BACK ON THE *OLD* LADY, BUT...
...BUT I'M NOT ENTIRE RESURED I CAN RECONNECT HOW TO *DO* IT ANYMORE.
"*YOU SEE, WE'VE BEEN WANDERLOST FOR SO LONG, AND WE'VE UNMEMBERED SO MUCH...*"

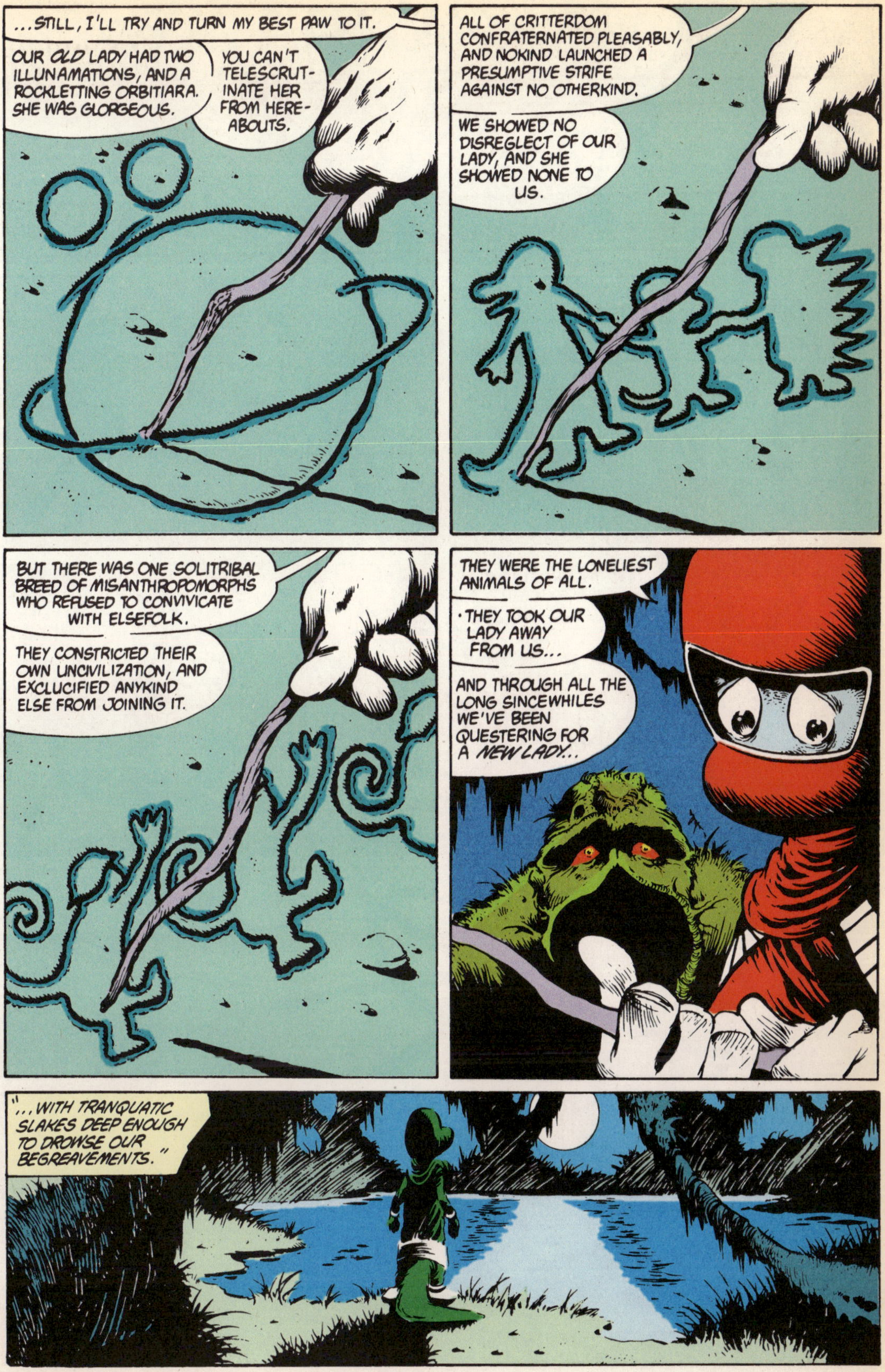
...STILL, I'LL TRY AND TURN MY BEST PAW TO IT.
OUR OLD LADY HAD TWO ILLUNAMATIONS, AND A ROCKLETTING ORBITIARA. SHE WAS GLORGEOUS.
YOU CAN'T TELESCRUT-INATE HER FROM HERE-ABOUTS.
ALL OF CRITTERDOM CONFRATERNATED PLEASABLY, AND NOKIND LAUNCHED A PRESUMPTIVE STRIFE AGAINST NO OTHERKIND.
WE SHOWED NO DISREGLECT OF OUR LADY, AND SHE SHOWED NONE TO US.
BUT THERE WAS ONE SOLITRIBAL BREED OF MISANTHROPOMORPHS WHO REFUSED TO CONVIVICATE WITH ELSEFOLK.
THEY CONSTRICTED THEIR OWN UNCIVILIZATION, AND EXCLUCIFIED ANYKIND ELSE FROM JOINING IT.
THEY WERE THE LONELIEST ANIMALS OF ALL.
THEY TOOK OUR LADY AWAY FROM US...
AND THROUGH ALL THE LONG SINCEWHILES WE'VE BEEN QUESTERING FOR A NEW LADY...
"...WITH TRANQUATIC SLAKES DEEP ENOUGH TO DROWSE OUR BEGREAVEMENTS."

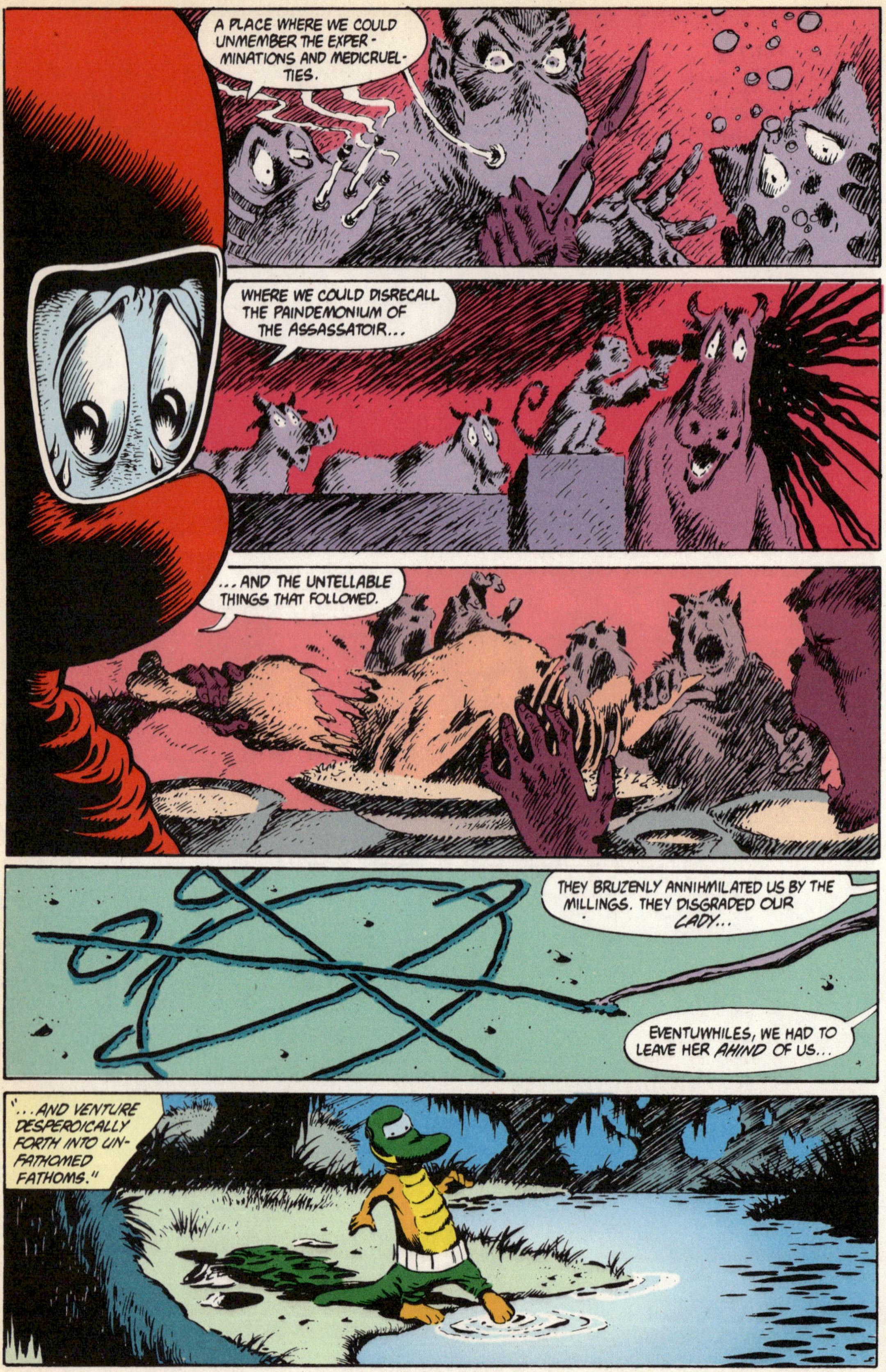
A PLACE WHERE WE COULD UNMEMBER THE EXPER-MINATIONS AND MEDICRUEL-TIES.
WHERE WE COULD DISRECALL THE PAINDEMONIUM OF THE ASSASSATOIR...
...AND THE UNTELLABLE THINGS THAT FOLLOWED.
THEY BRUZENLY ANNIHMILATED US BY THE MILLINGS. THEY DISGRADED OUR *LADY*...
EVENTUWHILES, WE HAD TO LEAVE HER *AHIND* OF US...
"...AND VENTURE DESPEROICALLY FORTH INTO UN-FATHOMED FATHOMS."

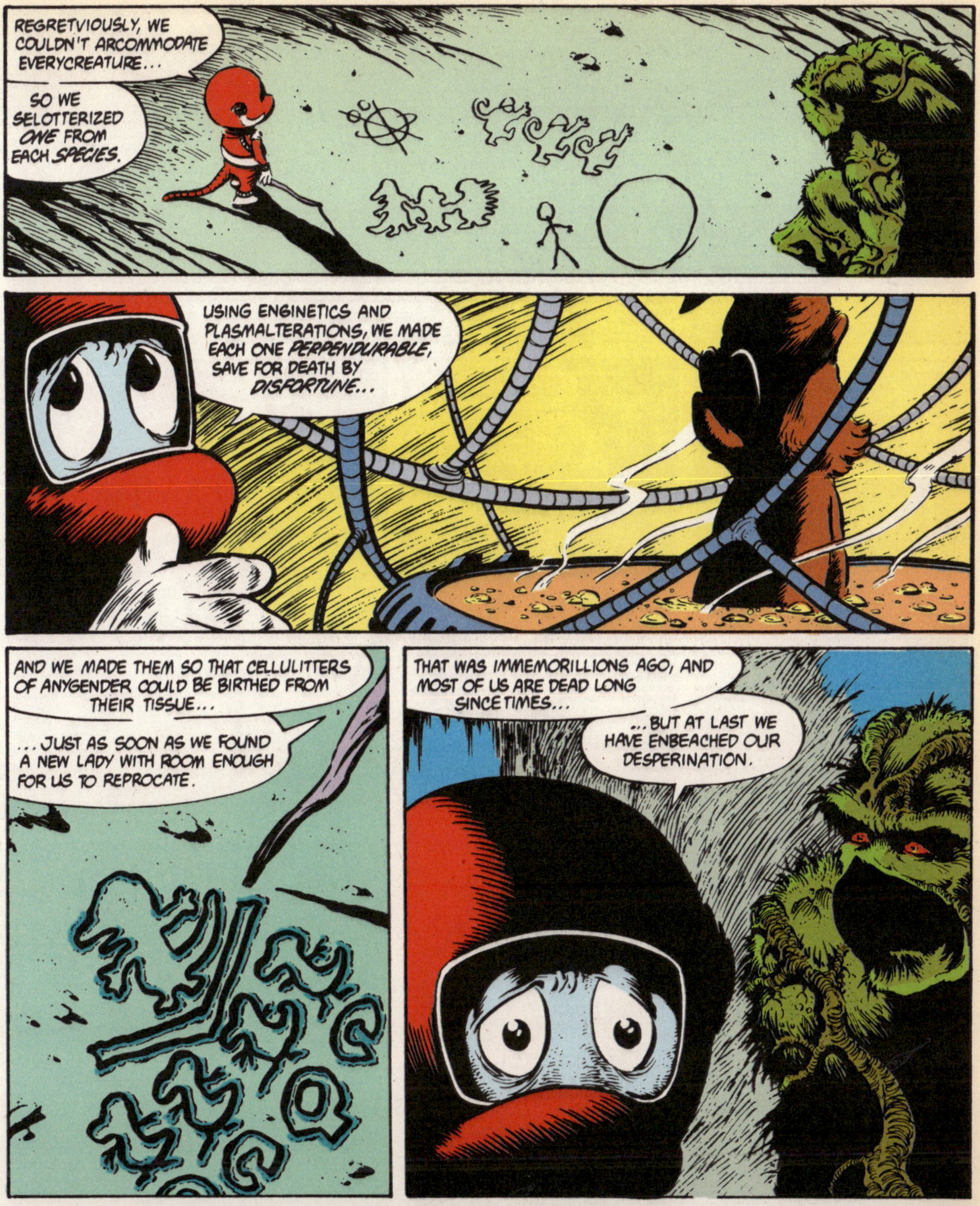
REGRETVIOUSLY, WE COULDN'T ARCOMMODATE EVERYCREATURE...
SO WE SELOTTERIZED ONE FROM EACH SPECIES.
USING ENGINETICS AND PLASMALTERATIONS, WE MADE EACH ONE PERPENDURABLE, SAVE FOR DEATH BY DISFORTUNE...
AND WE MADE THEM SO THAT CELLULITTERS OF ANYGENDER COULD BE BIRTHED FROM THEIR TISSUE...
...JUST AS SOON AS WE FOUND A NEW LADY WITH ROOM ENOUGH FOR US TO REPROCATE.
THAT WAS IMMEMORILLIONS AGO, AND MOST OF US ARE DEAD LONG SINCETIMES...
...BUT AT LAST WE HAVE ENBEACHED OUR DESPERINATION.
"AT LAST WE CAN REST."

...AND SO THAT'S... HMM?
WHY DID YOU UNSET YOURSELF?
ARE YOU GOING TO DEPASTURE FOR ELSEABOUTS, OR...?
YOU... WANT ME TO ESCOMPANY YOU?
YOU WANT TO DISVEIL SOMETHING TO ME?
WELL, ASSERTAINLY...
...BUT WE MUSTN'T BE UNHASTEFUL, OR MY KINLINGS WILL INFERE THAT YOU'VE UNSCAPED AND DISCORPSIFIED ME.
BATON ROUGE 1¾ MILES
RICHIE'S FARM
!

IS IT MUCH *DISTANTER?*
I'M A TARDLING COMPRIZED WITH YOU, AND NOT SO STRIDEFUL...
OH NO.
NOT *HERE* AS WELL.
THEY *CAN'T* OWN *THIS* LADY, TOO!
"WE WERE GOING TO BE HAPPY HERE."
DISPARANT CUZLINGS! LONG-LAST BROODLINGS! LET ME *ENGRACE* YOU!

"WH-WHY?
"WHY DIDN'T I REACH A REALITIZATION BEFOREWHILES?"
HOW CAN I TELL MY KINLINGS THAT I LET MYSELF BE SEDUPED BY A DISLUSION?
HOW CAN I TELL THE HYSTRICIDE THAT HE WAS RIGHT?
"THAT THERE IS NO LADY..."
...AND THAT IT WAS ALL JUST TRIFLES.
"TRIFLES LIGHT AS AIR."
YYYEEEEEEEEE

EEEEEEEEEEEEEEEE
BARTLE?

FROM THE LOG OF THE VIVI-QUINQUEREME "FIND THE LADY":
"THIS LADY HAS PREMONSTRATED HER INHOSPATILITY, AND FRONT-MATE BARTLE IS DEAD.
"WE CANNOT REBIDE IN THIS PLACE.

"I COULD SCAREFULLY BARE MYSELF TO TELL THE OTHERS.
"THE HYSTRICIDE, I THINK, WAS THE SOUL MOST ENSTRESSED BY MY DISPOSURE.
"HIS QUILLS BRINDLED, AND HE WOULD NOT LET US TOUCH THE CORPORELIC FOR SOME LITTLE TIME.
"OUR VIVI-QUINQUEREME PERFORMED THE NECROCESSARY EXGRAVATIONS...
"...AND THEN WE DELINQUISHED FRONT-MATE BARTLE TO THE SOIL HE HAD DIED BELIEVING WAS HIS HOME...
"...AND INFINALLY, IT WAS DONE...
"...SAVE FOR THE EXTINCT-SONG.

"'FIND THE LADY' DID HIS BETTERMOST NOT TO UNMEMBER THE WORDS, BUT I FEAR MOST OF THE SACREVERSES ARE LOST TO HIM.
"HE SANG 'DARK, A SOUL WIND BLASTS SO CHILLY...' LUCENTLY ENOUGH, BUT THE REST WAS MUMBLES.
"THE FLORALIEN CREATURE STOOD TO ATTENTIVENESS, ALTHOUGH I DOUBT IT WAS COMPREMOTION-ABLE TO HIM.
"AFTERWHILES, I THANKED HIM FOR HIS SINCERITABLE ATTITUDE.
"THEN WE WENT INBOARD AND ENSHELLTERED OURSELVES...
"...AND 'FIND THE LADY' RESTRACTED HIS CRANIMENTS...
"...AND DISCHARRED HIS ENTREACTORS...

"... AND WE CONTINUED ON OUR WAY."
--POG. (SHIPBOSS) AE: 8491. 4. 01.

SOPHISTICATED SUSPENSE
DC
75¢
33
FEB. 85
SWAMP THING®
TOTLEBEN
9-17-84

"MRS. CABLE?
"MRS. CABLE... THE APARTMENT IS YOURS, BUT I HAVE TO ASK A COUPLE OF QUESTIONS. IT SAYS HERE THAT YOU'RE MARRIED. WILL MR. CABLE BE LIVING HERE...?
"LIVING HERE...?
"LIVING HERE...?
"I'LL BE HONEST WITH YOU, MRS. CABLE... YOUR HUSBAND IS IN A DEEP COMA, AND THERE IS EVERY INDICATION THAT HE'S LIKELY TO STAY THAT WAY...
"STAY THAT WAY...
"STAY THAT WAY...
"ABBY... WE'RE ALL VERY SATISFIED WITH YOUR WORK HERE AT ELYSIUM LAWNS, BUT I WONDERED IF THINGS WERE OKAY WITH YOU PERSONALLY?
"I WANT TO HELP, ABBY, BUT WITH YOU IT'S ALL SECRETS AND MYSTERIES...
"SECRETS AND MYSTERIES
"SECRETS AND MYSTERIES
"SECRETS AND MYSTERIES"
ABANDONED HOUSES
RON RANDALL ARTIST
ALAN MOORE WRITER
COSTANZA LETTERER
WOOD COLORS
KAREN BERGER EDITOR

P-PRETTY SCARY PLACES, AREN'T THEY?
THEY STILL MAKE ME NERVOUS... AND I LIVE HERE.
WHAT I SAY IS, IF YOU CAN'T STAND THE COLD, KEEP OUT OF THE MORTUARY!

WHO ARE YOU?
AM I DREAMING THIS?
WELL, NOT EXACTLY... W-WE'RE A PROJECTION OF THE HUMAN UNCONSCIOUS, EXISTING AS A CONSTRUCT OF THE BRAIN'S RIGHT HEMISPHERE, AND...
IGNORE MY BROTHER. HE HAS NO SENSE OF MYSTERY.
YES. YOU'RE DREAMING THIS.
BUT...BUT...ARE YOU SUPPOSED TO KNOW THAT I'M DREAMING THIS? PEOPLE IN DREAMS DON'T USUALLY...
BANANA OIL! THEY PRETEND NOT TO KNOW TO AVOID EMBARRASSING YOU!
NOW HURRY UP AND CHOOSE!
CHOOSE?
YES... YOUR SUBCONSCIOUS HAS DIRECTED YOU HERE TO LEARN SOMETHING IMPORTANT, YOU SEE, AND...
ARE YOU LOOKING FOR A MYSTERY, OR A SECRET?
I...I DON'T KNOW. IS THERE A DIFFERENCE?
OF COURSE THERE'S A DIFFERENCE! MYSTERIES ARE WONDERS THAT YOU CAN PONDER AND SHARE. SECRETS ARE A BURDEN TO CARRY ALONE!
CHOOSE...
...BETWEEN MY HOUSE OF MYSTERY...
...AND MY BROTHER'S HOUSE OF SECRETS!

WELL...
IF IT'S ALL THE SAME TO YOU, I THINK I'D PREFER A GUIDED TOUR FROM YOUR BROTHER.
NOTHING PERSONAL.
YOUR LOSS, MY DEAR.
I-IS THAT ALL RIGHT? I MEAN, YOU WON'T BE ANGRY, WILL YOU? IF YOU'RE SURE THAT YOU DON'T MIND ME ESCORTING HER...
MIND? WHY SHOULD I MIND?
AM I YOUR KEEPER?
YOUR BROTHER SEEMS PRETTY ABRASIVE. DOESN'T HE GET ON YOUR NERVES?
WELL, HE'S NOT SO BAD. HE JUST GETS JEALOUS WHEN PEOPLE LIKE ME BETTER THAN HIM, I SUPPOSE.
BUT YOU'RE RIGHT...
SOMETIMES HE CAN BE MURDER.
THROUGH HERE.

IT'S VERY STRANGE AND CLUTTERED...
YES, YOU'RE RIGHT... THIS IS THE PART OF THE UNCONSCIOUS WHERE ALL THE STORIES ARE BORN AND KEPT.
THERE ARE TOO MANY TO KEEP TIDY, ALTHOUGH GOD KNOWS I TRY...
OVER THERE'S A STORY ABOUT AN OLD WOMAN WHO KEPT THE OCEAN IN A BOTTLE.
DOWN HERE'S THE TALE OF AN ORCHARD THAT BORE SKULLS INSTEAD OF FRUIT. ALL TRUE, YOU KNOW...
THIS WAY...
THERE'S A LOT OF DUST...
HMMM. WELL, THINGS HAVE BEEN QUIET AROUND HERE THESE LAST FEW YEARS. PEOPLE DON'T DROP BY SO MUCH. I THINK THAT'S WHAT ANNOYS MY BROTHER. BEING NEGLECTED...
DOWN HERE...
LISTEN, ARE YOU SURE I'M GOING TO LEARN SOMETHING IMPORTANT FROM ALL THIS...?
OH, YES! MOST CERTAINLY! I'VE GOT A VERY SPECIAL SECRET BACK HERE SOME-PLACE THAT'S JUST FOR YOU!
NOW, WHERE DID I...
AHH!
HERE IT IS!

A BRACELET?
BRACELET?
OH, NO! NO, IT JUST LOOKS LIKE A BRACELET. IT'S REALLY A STORY. A SPECIAL CIRCULAR STORY THAT GOES ROUND AND ROUND...
BUT WHAT DOES IT HAVE TO DO WITH ME?
AHHH! NOW, THAT'S THE SECRET!
YOU'RE NOT AN ORDINARY WOMAN, YOU KNOW. SOME STRANGE STORIES HAVE INTRUDED UPON YOUR LIFE LATELY...
STORIES? EVERYTHING THAT'S HAPPENED TO ME HAS BEEN REAL...
OH, PLEASE, IT WAS JUST A FIGURE OF SPEECH. DON'T TAKE OFFENSE. YOU SEE, IN A WAY, EVERYTHING IS MADE OF STORIES.
HERE... DO SIT DOWN...
YOU SEE, WHAT I'M GETTING AT IS, THESE THINGS THAT HAVE HAPPENED TO YOU!...
...THEY'VE ALL HAPPENED BEFORE, IN SIMILAR CIRCUMSTANCES!
IT'S LIKE A CIRCLE. IT GOES ROUND AND ROUND AND ROUND...
I'M SORRY, BUT THIS SOUNDS LOONY. I BETTER GO...
OH, NO! PLEASE! YOU MUST LISTEN TO THE STORY...
IT'S ONE OF MY FAVORITES.
IT STARTS LIKE THIS...
"I CANNOT REMEMBER THE MORNING ANYMORE..."

I CANNOT REMEMBER THE MORNING ANYMORE--BUT I KNOW THE EVENING WELL! I BELONG TO IT NOW--AND IT CARES FOR ME IN RETURN--SHELTERING ME--NURTURING ME, HOLDING ME CLOSE WITHIN ITS VELVET EMBRACE...
THE MOON IS RISING NOW, CLAWING ITS WAY INTO THE SKY--A GLOWING, AMBER EYE THAT CASTS ITS DISDAINFUL GAZE ON THE MURKY OOZE BELOW--THE SWAMP THAT IS MY HOME...
I MOVE SLOWLY THROUGH THE MOSS-DRAPED MIRE--TREADING A PATH THAT IS WORN SMOOTH FROM MY CONSTANT PASSING--ON BEYOND THE SHADOWS AND THE DARK TREES' TWISTING TENDRILS TO MY INEVITABLE DESTINATION...
THE EDGE OF THE SWAMP--AND THE MIST-WET OLD MANSION THAT RISES LIKE AN AGING APPARITION INTO A COLD EXPANSE OF SKY--A STATELY SANCTUARY FULL OF BRIGHT LIGHTS AND PROMISES--AND MEMORIES THAT BRING ONLY PAIN...
STORY: LEN WEIN
ART: BERNI WRIGHTSON
SWAMP THING

I HAVE STOOD WATCHING THAT OLD GRAY EDIFICE FOR MORE LONELY NIGHTS THAN I WANT TO RECALL -- DREAMING ENDLESSLY OF THE SOFT GOLDEN LADY WHO LIVES WITHIN -- KNOWING I CAN NEVER HAVE HER -- WONDERING WHAT SHE'S DOING NOW...
YOU SMILE BECAUSE HE EXPECTS YOU TO--BUT IN THE SHADOWED CORRIDORS OF YOUR HEART THERE IS NO REAL JOY--THERE NEVER CAN BE...
A TOAST, MY DARLING--TO US! TODAY IS SIX MONTHS SINCE WE WERE WED!
YOUR NAME IS LINDA OLSEN RIDGE--AND YOUR MIND IS A RAGING RIVER THIS NIGHT--CARRYING YOUR THOUGHTS ALONG A SURGING STREAM OF CONSCIOUSNESS--SENDING MEMORIES CRASHING LIKE WAVES UPON SOME DISTANT SHORE...
YOU'RE THINKING ABOUT ALEX AGAIN, AREN'T YOU, DARLING? I CAN SEE IT IN YOUR EYES!
I'M SORRY, DAMIAN-- IT'S JUST THAT HE'S STILL SO REAL TO ME!
LINDA, ALEX OLSEN IS DEAD --AND YOU ARE MY WIFE NOW! EVENTUALLY, YOU WILL HAVE TO REALIZE THAT FACT! ALEX IS GONE, DARLING--THERE IS NOTHING TO DO BUT FORGET HIM!
NEVER-- FOR TO FORGET ALEX OLSEN IS TO DENY A PART OF YOURSELF--A GOOD PART--FILLED WITH HAPPY SUMMER DAYS AND STAR-DAPPLED NIGHTS-- MIST COVERS YOUR EYES--AND MEMORIES FALL WITH THE TEARS...

WHAT IS A MEMORY? IT IS RIBBONS... CANDLES... A PARTY! YOU HAVE BEEN ALEX'S WIFE FOR TWELVE SHORT MONTHS... IT SEEMS LIKE ONLY YESTERDAY...
HAPPY ANNIVERSARY TO MY TWO DEAREST FRIENDS! I REALLY ENVY YOU, ALEX! YOU GOT YOURSELF QUITE A PRIZE IN LINDA!
AND DON'T THINK I DON'T KNOW IT!
AN ANNIVERSARY GIFT, DARLING-- FOR YOU! A SYMBOL OF MY FEELING FOR YOU!
A GOLDEN BRACELET! LINDA, I... I'LL NEVER TAKE IT OFF AS LONG AS I LIVE! I PROMISE YOU THAT!
WHAT IS A MEMORY? IT IS THE FEELING OF PRIDE YOU HAVE BEING MARRIED TO A FAST-RISING YOUNG SCIENTIST WITH THE WORLD AT HIS DOORSTEP...
WE MAKE A FINE TEAM, DAMIAN-- I DON'T KNOW WHERE I'D BE WITHOUT YOUR HELP!
IF THIS PROJECT SUCCEEDS, ALEX-- THAT WILL BE ALL THE THANKS I NEED!
WHAT IS A MEMORY? IT IS THE SEARING SOUND OF DEVASTATION-- AS YOU WATCH YOUR WORLD GO UP IN FLAMES BEFORE YOU...
OH, DEAR GOD--NO! ALEX'S LAB...
WARAROOOM!
WHAT IS A MEMORY? IT IS THE GAPING WOUND THAT ONCE HAD BEEN YOUR HEART--WHEN YOU LEARN YOU ARE ALONE...
DON'T GO IN THERE! THERE'S NOTHING LEFT TO SEE, LINDA! ALEX IS DEAD!
OH, DAMIAN, NO... NO... NO... NO... NO...

WHAT IS A MEMORY? IT IS A FLEETING FANTASY FAR TOO PAINFUL TO LONG REMAIN--THAT CARRIES YOU BACK THROUGH THE PORTAL OF THE PAST TO THE HARSH REALITY OF NOW...
LINDA, YOU HAVEN'T HEARD A WORD I'VE SAID!
I'M SORRY, DARLING--MY MIND WAS WANDERING--FORGIVE ME!
A HOLLOW RAIN HAS BEGUN TO FALL --AS COLD AND EMPTY AS THE ACHING DEEP WITHIN ME--I CAN BEAR IT NO LONGER--THE GRIM, GRAY MANOR STANDS STARK AGAINST THE NIGHT, MOCKING ME--I BEGIN TO MOVE...
THE NIGHT HAS GROWN COLDER NOW--YOU CAN FEEL IT CROUCHED IN THE DARKNESS--WAITING FOR YOU...
IS SOMETHING WRONG, LINDA? YOU DON'T SEEM WELL!
ONLY THE CHILL NIGHT AIR, DARLING--IT WILL PASS!
YOU LOOK INTO YOUR HUSBAND'S EYES--AND YOU SEE ONLY SHADOWS--DARK, VEILED THINGS THAT WHISPER TO THE SURFACE--AND QUICKLY FADE AWAY--AND YOU WONDER WHAT IS GOING THROUGH HIS MIND...
DEAR, SWEET LINDA--HOW TRULY LOVELY YOU REALLY ARE!
"I NEVER REALLY FORGAVE ALEX FOR MARRYING YOU WHEN HE KNEW HOW MUCH I LOVED YOU--YOU'LL NEVER KNOW HOW HARD IT WAS FOR ME TO KEEP UP THE FACADE OF THE 'ETERNAL FRIEND'..."
HAPPY ANNIVERSARY TO MY TWO DEAREST FRIENDS!

"TO SEE YOU EVERY DAY--SO CLOSE AND YET SO IMPOSSIBLY DISTANT--NEVER TO KNOW YOUR TOUCH OR THE FRAGRANCE OF YOUR HAIR--IT WAS MORE THAN I COULD BEAR..."
"IT WAS I WHO ARRANGED THE EXPLOSION--ALONE AT NIGHT IN ALEX'S DARKENED LABORATORY--QUIETLY ALTERING THE VITAL COMPONENTS--TO RID MYSELF OF THE ONLY OBSTACLE IN MY WAY--MY BEST FRIEND..."
"YOU'LL NEVER KNOW THAT ALEX WASN'T KILLED IN THE EXPLOSION--THAT I CARRIED HIS BATTERED AND BLOODY FORM OUT INTO THE FETID INTERIOR OF THE SWAMP BEYOND--AND BURIED IT THERE..."
I WAS EVERY BIT THE BEREAVED FRIEND AT THE FUNERAL--ALWAYS THE COMFORTING SHOULDER--THE TENDER WORD--IT WAS ONLY A MATTER OF TIME UNTIL YOU TURNED TO ME FOR COMFORT--OUR MARRIAGE WAS INEVITABLE!
FORGIVE ME, DARLING--BUT THE CHILL HAS GROWN WORSE! PERHAPS I OUGHT TO RETIRE TO MY ROOM!
OF COURSE, LINDA--HOW THOUGHTLESS OF ME! GO AHEAD... I'LL JOIN YOU SHORTLY!

YOU WALK QUIETLY DOWN THE CORRIDOR TO THE SHELTER OF YOUR ROOM-- AND YOU CAN FEEL DAMIAN'S GAZE FOLLOWING YOU-- SEARING TREMORS INTO THE SMALL OF YOUR BACK...
SHE CAN'T BEAR MY TOUCH ANYMORE-- THAT'S THE FIRST SIGN! ALL THE LITTLE SCRAPS OF INFORMATION SHE'S BEEN GATHERING ARE COMING TOGETHER AT LAST!
IT'S ONLY A MATTER OF TIME BEFORE SHE REALIZES THAT I KILLED ALEX--AND THAT WILL MEAN MY END! HOWEVER MUCH I CARE FOR LINDA, MY OWN NECK COMES FIRST... LINDA MUST DIE!
THE CANDLES THAT LIGHT YOUR ROOM PROVIDE THE ONLY REAL WARMTH YOU'VE FELT THIS NIGHT--BUT EVEN THROUGH THAT MELLOW GLOW, THE CHILL RETURNS ONCE MORE...
DAMIAN IS HALF-WAY ACROSS THE HOUSE,.. WHY CAN'T I SHAKE THE FEELING THAT SOMEONE IS WATCHING ME?
MY HEART BEATS SOFTLY ONCE AGAIN--FOR THE SPARKLE IN HER EYES FILLS MY SOUL WITH A JOY I CANNOT DESERVE--LINDA-- HER NAME RINGS LIKE FINE CRYSTAL-- HER HAIR SHINES LIKE GOLD...
LINDA? ARE YOU FEELING BETTER, DARLING?
A LITTLE BETTER, I SUPPOSE, DAMIAN... BUT DON'T WORRY YOURSELF-- IT REALLY IS NOTHING!
NONSENSE! COME-- I'LL MASSAGE YOUR NECK--THAT SHOULD WORK OUT THE CHILL!
I WATCH DAMIAN RIDGE WALK SOFTLY ACROSS THE RUG AND SOMETHING GLITTERS IN HIS HAND-- A HYPODERMIC NEEDLE!

HE STANDS SILENTLY BEHIND HER, THE NEEDLE POISED TO STRIKE -- TO END THE LIFE OF THE ONLY THING IN THIS WORLD THAT MAKES MY EXISTENCE BEARABLE -- THE ONLY REASON I LIVE -- FURY FILLS THE SPACES BEHIND MY EYES -- AND I WALK INTO THE ROOM...
OH, GOD-- NO!
CRRASSHHHH!
WITH A SPEED I HAVE NEVER KNOWN BEFORE, I MOVE THE FETID BULK THAT IS MY BODY ACROSS THE SPAN OF FEET -- AND THE CLAW THAT IS MY HAND CLOSES UPON DAMIAN'S WRIST -- CRUSHING IT...
GET AWAY-- GET AWAY FROM... ARRRGGHH!
SLOWLY -- CERTAINLY -- I FORCE THE LIFE FROM DAMIAN'S BLACK-HEARTED BODY -- A LIFE HE DOES NOT DESERVE...
FOR SEVERAL SHORT MINUTES, DAMIAN RIDGE STRUGGLES FOR HIS UNWORTHY LIFE -- TEARING, CLAWING, RIPPING DECAYING SHREDS FROM WHAT ONCE HAD BEEN MY FLESH -- UNTIL, AT LAST, HE LIES STILL -- FOREVER...
...AND MY BRIGHT, GOLDEN LADY STANDS SCREAMING BEHIND ME...

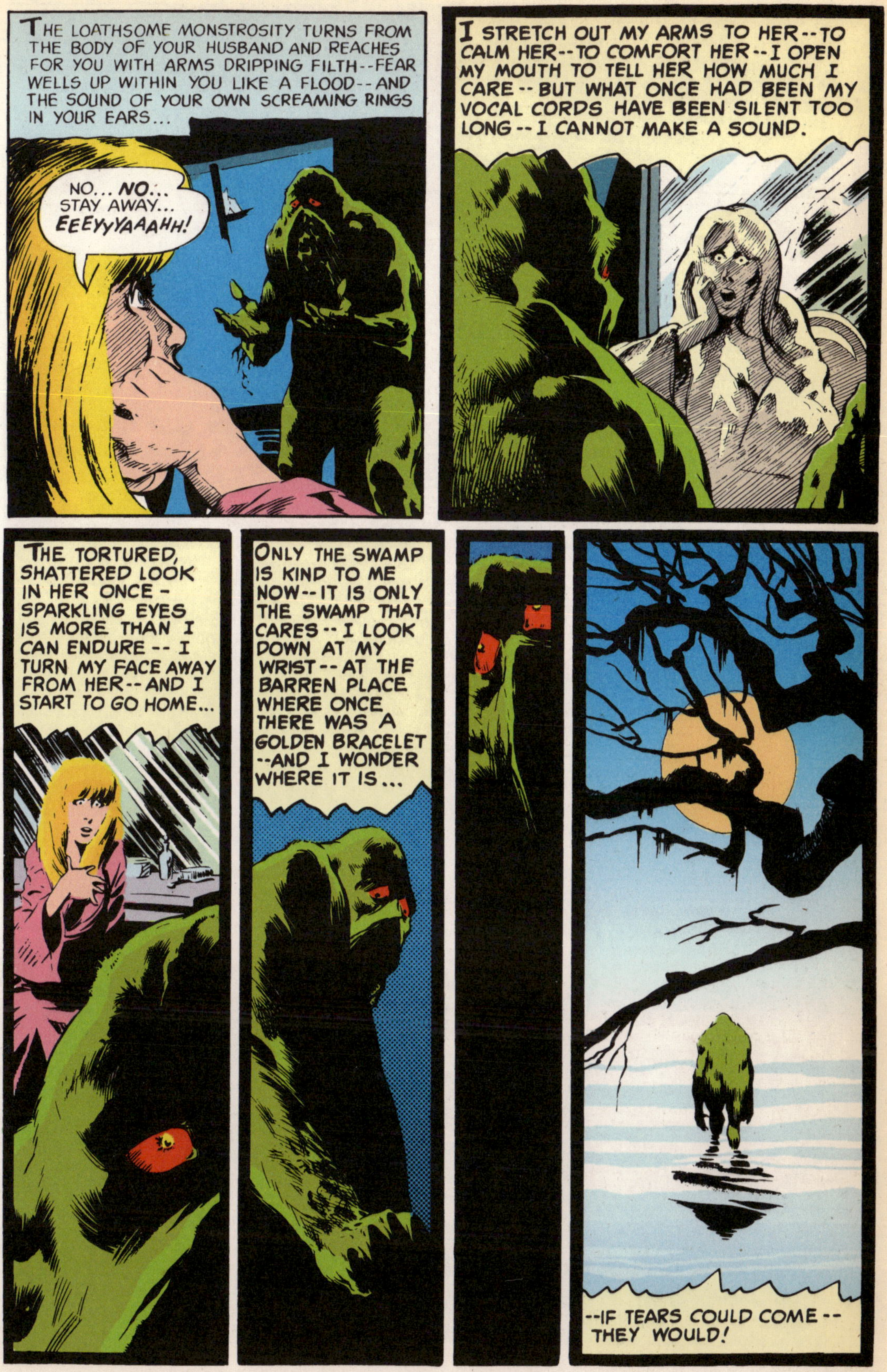
THE LOATHSOME MONSTROSITY TURNS FROM THE BODY OF YOUR HUSBAND AND REACHES FOR YOU WITH ARMS DRIPPING FILTH--FEAR WELLS UP WITHIN YOU LIKE A FLOOD--AND THE SOUND OF YOUR OWN SCREAMING RINGS IN YOUR EARS...
NO... NO... STAY AWAY... EEEYYYAAAHH!
I STRETCH OUT MY ARMS TO HER--TO CALM HER--TO COMFORT HER--I OPEN MY MOUTH TO TELL HER HOW MUCH I CARE--BUT WHAT ONCE HAD BEEN MY VOCAL CORDS HAVE BEEN SILENT TOO LONG--I CANNOT MAKE A SOUND.
THE TORTURED, SHATTERED LOOK IN HER ONCE-SPARKLING EYES IS MORE THAN I CAN ENDURE--I TURN MY FACE AWAY FROM HER--AND I START TO GO HOME...
ONLY THE SWAMP IS KIND TO ME NOW--IT IS ONLY THE SWAMP THAT CARES--I LOOK DOWN AT MY WRIST--AT THE BARREN PLACE WHERE ONCE THERE WAS A GOLDEN BRACELET--AND I WONDER WHERE IT IS...
--IF TEARS COULD COME--THEY WOULD!

"...AND IF TEARS COULD COME, THEY WOULD."
THE END.
THERE...A SAD LITTLE STORY, ISN'T IT?
BUT... BUT THAT'S ALEC'S STORY!
ALEC HOLLAND... NOT ALEX OLSEN! AND IT DIDN'T HAPPEN AT THE TURN OF THE CENTURY...IT HAPPENED DECADES LATER!
LOOK, WHAT IS THIS?
IT'S THE SECRET! THE SECRET YOU CAME TO LEARN!
ALEC HOLLAND WAS NOT THE FIRST THING TO WALK THE SWAMPS!
THERE WERE OTHERS BEFORE HIM.
BUT...THAT'S IMPOSSIBLE. EVEN ALLOWING FOR COINCIDENCE...
NO! NOT COINCIDENCE! DESIGN!
IN THE HISTORY OF THE WORLD, THERE HAVE COME SOUR TIMES WHEN THE EARTH FEELS COMPELLED TO CREATE AN ELEMENTAL CHAMPION FOR ITSELF.
BUT ALEC'S TRANSFORMATION WAS AN ACCIDENT...
THERE ARE NO ACCIDENTS. SOUR TIMES ARE RETURNING TO YOUR WORLD, AND YOUR WORLD HAS AGAIN SHAPED A PROTECTOR TO STAND AGAINST THEM.
THAT IS WHAT YOU CAME TO LEARN!
NOW FORGIVE ME, BUT IF THE WARNING IS TO BE ANY USE TO YOU, WE MUST HURRY..
HURRY? BUT WHY? I DON'T UNDERSTAND...

MY BROTHER! IF I CAN SNEAK YOU OUT BEFORE HE THINKS TO CHECK ON OUR WHEREABOUTS, EVERYTHING WILL BE ALL RIGHT...
LOOK, PLEASE, I REALLY CAN'T FOLLOW THIS. IT DOESN'T MAKE SENSE...
IT'S MY FAULT. I'M SO BAD AT EXPLAINING THINGS...
JUST REMEMBER THE STORY OF ALEX OLSEN. TELL YOUR SWAMP THING THE TALE AS I TOLD IT TO YOU...
THEN, WHEN THE TROUBLE STARTS, IT WILL HELP HIM UNDERSTAND HIS PLACE IN THE SCHEME OF THINGS.
IT ISN'T MUCH, BUT IT'S THE BEST I CAN DO.
THROUGH HERE...
MY BROTHER'S PROBABLY BUSY FEEDING HIS GARGOYLES RIGHT NOW...
IF YOU GO ACROSS THE GROUNDS AND OUT THROUGH THE GATE, YOU'LL MAKE IT BACK TO WAKEFULNESS WITH THE SECRET INTACT AND READY TO PASS ON...
...BUT THEN IT WOULDN'T BE A SECRET, WOULD IT?
YOU KNOW THE RULES, BROTHER...
...AND NOW YOU MUST PAY THE FORFEIT.

BUT... SHE MUST BE ALLOWED TO TAKE THE STORY WITH HER WHEN SHE LEAVES. HER WORLD IS IN DANGER...
IF SHE WANTED SOMETHING SHE COULD SHARE WITH OTHERS, SHE SHOULD HAVE CHOSEN A MYSTERY...
...FOR SECRETS MUST BE KEPT FOREVER. I WARNED HER...
I...I WON'T LET YOU DO THIS! IT'S JUST BECAUSE YOU'RE JEALOUS...
YOU'VE ALWAYS BEEN JEALOUS!
JEALOUS? OF YOU?
NO... I AM SIMPLY DISGUSTED. WE HAVE BEEN CHARGED, YOU AND I, WITH THE SAFEKEEPING OF THE STORIES. WHO BETTER? WE WERE IN THE FIRST STORY...
NOW YOU WOULD BETRAY THAT TRUST.
WHEN THE WOMAN LEAVES HERE SHE WILL FORGET YOUR LITTLE YARN. IT WILL REMAIN SAFE IN SOME BACKWATER OF HER MIND, IGNORED AS A SECRET SHOULD BE...
NO! I WON'T LET YOU!
UPH!
GET OFF OF ME, YOU OBESE SLUG...
I'M WARNING YOU...
GET OFF BEFORE I...

CAIN! NO!
NOT AGAIN!
RUNCH
RUNCH RUNCH
YOU... YOU MURDERED HIM.
YOUR OWN BROTHER...
MURDER? DON'T TALK TO ME ABOUT MURDER!
I INVENTED MURDER!

AS FOR THAT FAT OAF, DON'T WORRY ABOUT HIM. HE'LL BE UP AND ABOUT TOMORROW, BUMBLING AROUND JUST AS GOOD AS NEW...
...AT LEAST UNTIL THE NEXT TIME.
IT'S ALL WE HAVE TO DO NOW THAT NOBODY WANTS TO HEAR THE STORIES ANYMORE.
THE SAME ACT OVER AND OVER AGAIN...
IT'S OUR PUNISHMENT, FOR DOING IT THE FIRST TIME.
BUT WHY SHOULD YOU BOTH BE PUNISHED FOR SOMETHING THAT YOU DID? IT ISN'T FAIR!
OF COURSE IT'S FAIR! I'M BEING PUNISHED FOR BEING THE FIRST PREDATOR...
...AND HE'S BEING PUNISHED FOR BEING THE FIRST VICTIM.
NOW... I THINK IT'S TIME FOR YOU TO LEAVE.
REMEMBER TO TAKE YOUR SECRET WITH YOU. TOO BAD THAT YOU WON'T BE ABLE TO SHARE IT WITH ANYBODY.
WAIT! DON'T LEAVE ME HERE!
HOW CAN I SEE WHERE I'M GOING IN THIS FOG?
HOW AM I SUPPOSED TO FIND MY WAY...
...HOME?

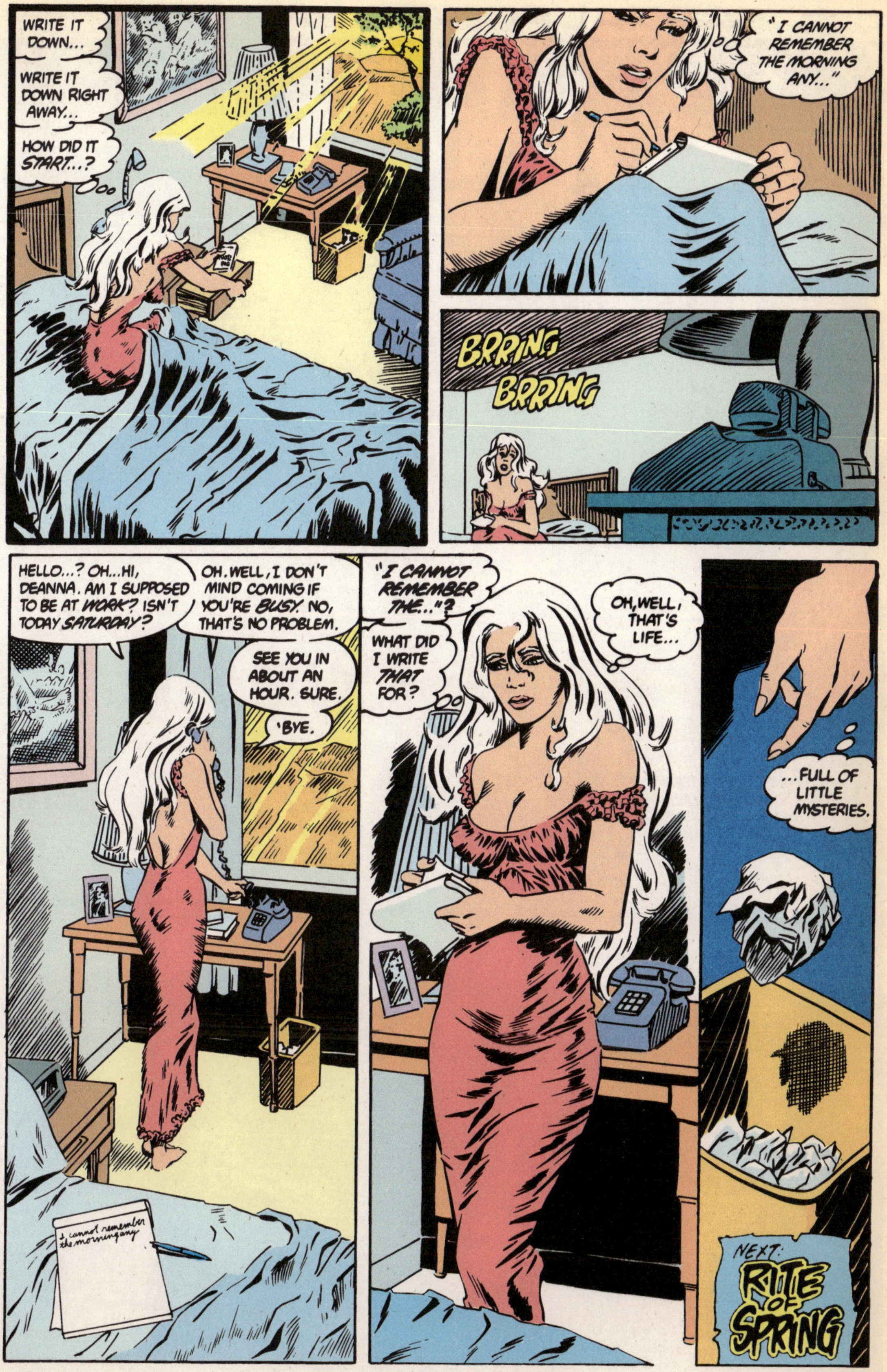
WRITE IT DOWN...
WRITE IT DOWN RIGHT AWAY...
HOW DID IT START...?
"I CANNOT REMEMBER THE MORNING ANY..."
BRRING
BRRING
HELLO...? OH...HI, DEANNA. AM I SUPPOSED TO BE AT WORK? ISN'T TODAY SATURDAY?
OH. WELL, I DON'T MIND COMING IF YOU'RE BUSY. NO, THAT'S NO PROBLEM.
SEE YOU IN ABOUT AN HOUR. SURE.
'BYE.
I cannot remember the morning any
"I CANNOT REMEMBER THE..."?
WHAT DID I WRITE THAT FOR?
OH, WELL, THAT'S LIFE...
...FULL OF LITTLE MYSTERIES.
NEXT: RITE OF SPRING

SPECIAL POSTER GALLERY

SPECIAL POSTER GALLERY

SPECIAL POSTER GALLERY

75¢
34
MAR. 85
SWAMP THING
BY
ALAN MOORE, STEPHEN BISSETTE AND JOHN TOTLEBEN

SPRING CAME, AND EVERYTHING IN THE WORLD WOKE UP...
TERREBONNE PARISH GENERAL HOSPITAL
...EXCEPT HIM.
CAUTION
OXYGEN TENT IN USE
OUTSIDE, THE RUDE YOUNG TENDRILS, SUPPLE AND GREEN, MUSCLED UPWARD THROUGH CHINKS IN THE TURF'S DARK UNDERBELLY.
THE DOCTOR SAID THERE WAS LITTLE INDICATION OF HIGHER BRAIN ACTIVITY. HE WAS NOT EXPECTED TO RECOVER.
YES, SHE FELT GUILTY, FELT RELIEVED, FRIGHTENED, ANGRY, ALL THOSE THINGS...
...BUT THE SEPARATE SHADES OF HER GRIEF HAD MERGED, LIKE VIVID MODELING-CLAYS CRUSHED TOGETHER, INTO A SINGLE MAUVE-BROWN BRUISE.
BRUISES FADE EVENTUALLY.
THE DOCTOR VENTURED THAT SUCH A BEAUTIFUL YOUNG WOMAN, HER LIFE AHEAD OF HER, WOULD SOON FIND SOMEONE ELSE.
OUTSIDE, BEES JERKED THROUGH THE GLASSY AFTERNOON, THEIR HIND LEGS DIPPED IN POWDERED GOLD.
THEY'D SPRAYED THE PLANTS IN THE LOBBY. DIAMONDS OF PERSPIRATION GLISTENED ON SKINS OF COOL AND BURNISHED GREEN.
RUIZ
SHE FELT AN ACHE, BUT NOT OF MOURNING.
SHE KNEW WHO SHE WANTED TO BE WITH.

CREATED BY LEN WEIN
SWAMP THING
AND BERNI WRIGHTSON
RITE of SPRING
ALAN MOORE
WRITER
STEPHEN BISSETTE & JOHN TOTLEBEN
ARTISTS
KAREN BERGER
EDITOR
TATJANA WOOD
COLORIST
JOHN COSTANZA
LETTERER

DO YOU MIND IF I...?
NO.
PLEASE... TAKE IT...
Y'KNOW... THE WAY YOU LOOK...
I THINK I LIKE YOU BEST IN SPRING.

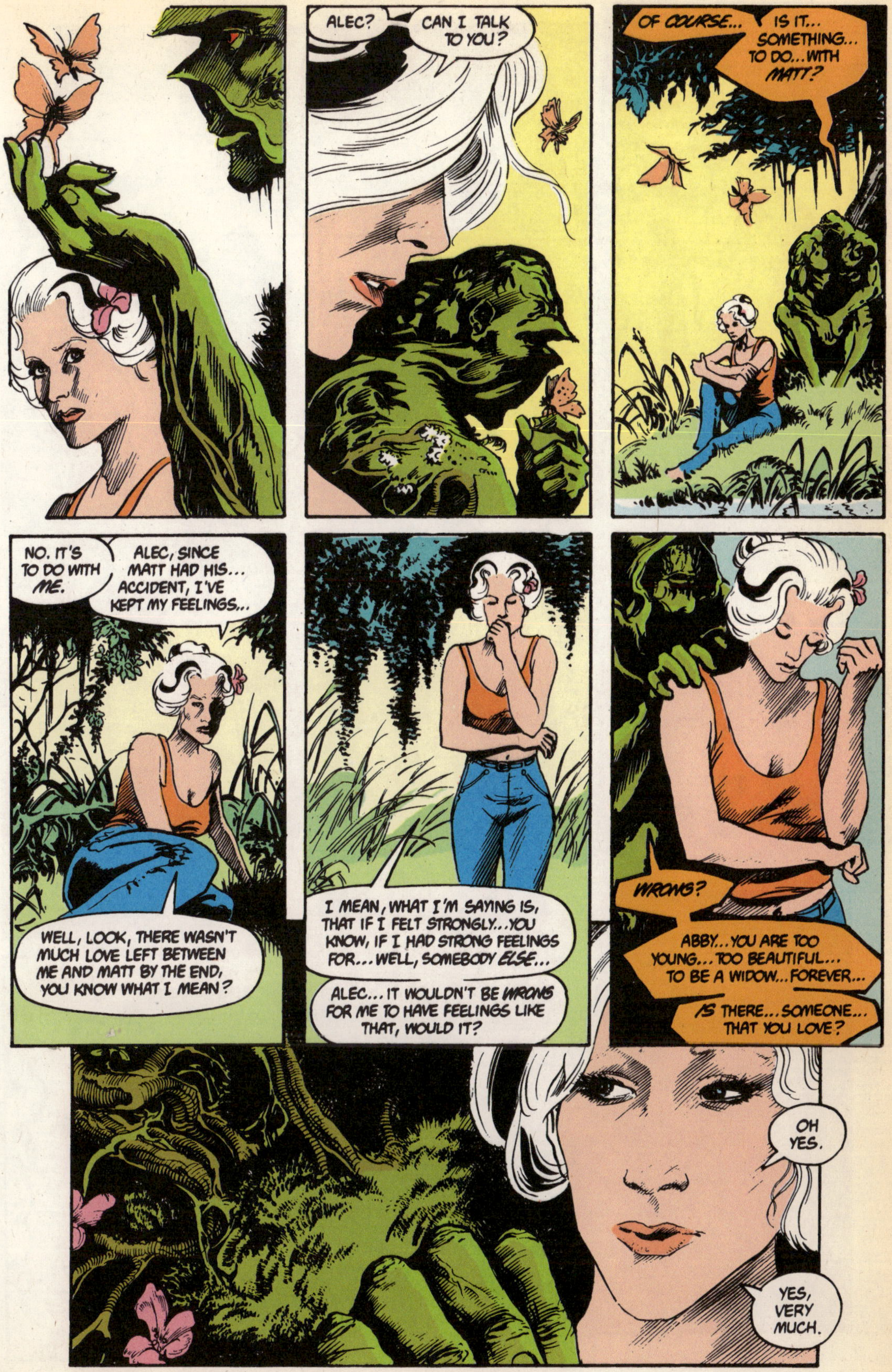
ALEC?
CAN I TALK TO YOU?
OF COURSE...
IS IT... SOMETHING... TO DO... WITH MATT?
NO. IT'S TO DO WITH ME.
ALEC, SINCE MATT HAD HIS... ACCIDENT, I'VE KEPT MY FEELINGS...
WELL, LOOK, THERE WASN'T MUCH LOVE LEFT BETWEEN ME AND MATT BY THE END, YOU KNOW WHAT I MEAN?
I MEAN, WHAT I'M SAYING IS, THAT IF I FELT STRONGLY... YOU KNOW, IF I HAD STRONG FEELINGS FOR... WELL, SOMEBODY ELSE...
ALEC... IT WOULDN'T BE WRONG FOR ME TO HAVE FEELINGS LIKE THAT, WOULD IT?
WRONG?
ABBY... YOU ARE TOO YOUNG... TOO BEAUTIFUL... TO BE A WIDOW... FOREVER...
IS THERE... SOMEONE... THAT YOU LOVE?
OH YES.
YES, VERY MUCH.

THEN... YOU MUST NOT... TORTURE YOURSELF... WITH POINTLESS GUILT...
IF... THERE IS... SOMEONE... THAT YOU LOVE... THEN TELL THEM...
YEAH, WELL...
THAT'S, Y'KNOW...
THAT'S WHAT I'M TRYING TO DO.
YOU MEAN...
...ME...?
OH, FOR GOD'S SAKE...
WHO ELSE?

OH NO.
I'VE RUINED IT, HAVEN'T I? I'VE SCREWED IT UP...
I SHOULD NEVER HAVE SAID...
LOOK...LET'S JUST FORGET IT. I'LL GO HOME NOW, AND WE'LL FORGET I SAID ANYTHING.
I MEAN, IT'S JUST SO RIDICULOUS, RIGHT? IT'S IMPOSSIBLE, IT'S BIZARRE, IT PROBABLY ISN'T EVEN LEGAL...
OH HELL.
THERE'S SOMETHING WRONG WITH ME. I BUILD THINGS UP IN MY MIND...
I READ THINGS INTO THE WAY YOU LOOK AT ME, KID MYSELF THAT MAYBE YOU FEEL THE SAME AS I DO, BUT...
YOU'RE A PLANT, FOR GOD'S SAKE!
JUST SAYING IT OUT LOUD, I MEAN, IT'S JUST SO FUNNY!
HOW COULD YOU LOVE ME?
DEEPLY...
SILENTLY...
...AND...FOR TOO MANY... YEARS.
YOU...
YOU NEVER SAID.
NO. I THOUGHT... IT WOULD... FRIGHTEN YOU..
ABBY...?
WHAT...DO WE DO...NOW?
I'VE... NEVER KISSED YOU...
IT...WOULD BE...UNPLEASANT FOR YOU. ABBY...WE ARE SO...DIFFERENT...

OH.
IT'S LIKE LIME, BUT...
...BUT NOT AS SHARP.

DO...
DO YOU... LIKE... LIME?
IT'S MY FAVORITE.
YOU WANT TO WALK FOR A WHILE?
ABBY...?
YES?
YOU... ARE HUMAN...
YOU NEED... MORE FROM LOVE...
...THAN THE TASTE... OF LIME...
UH...
YOU'RE UH...
YOU'RE TALKING ABOUT... ABOUT SEX, RIGHT?

WELL, LISTEN...
I MEAN, I HAVE, Y'KNOW, THOUGHT ABOUT ALL THAT, BUT...
I MEAN, I KNOW THAT... THE PHYSICAL SIDE OF THINGS... I KNOW THAT'S NOT POSSIBLE, BUT...
LOOK, WHAT I'M SAYING IS THAT IT'S NOT IMPORTANT. NOT TO ME.
AS LONG AS ALL THE OTHER STUFF IS THERE. AS LONG AS YOU... WELL, WANT ME, I GUESS, AND SORT OF CARE ABOUT ME...
BUT THERE... SHOULD BE... SOME FORM... OF COMMUNION...
POK

YEAH. YEAH, I KNOW, BUT...
...BUT IT DOESN'T HAVE TO BE PHYSICAL.
NO.
PLEASE...
WAIT HERE... FOR A MOMENT...
UH...
WHAT YOU WANT ME TO, UH...
WHAT, YOU MEAN, LIKE, I'M SUPPOSED TO, UH...
...EAT IT?

YES.
DOES... THE IDEA... *REPEL* YOU...?
N-NO, NOT ANY-*MORE*...
THE FIRST TIME... THE FIRST TIME I THOUGHT ABOUT SOMEBODY *EATING* PART OF YOU, I...
WELL, I THREW UP.
BUT... IF THIS IS LIKE, SOMETHING THAT YOU *WANT* ME TO DO...
GMNMM...
THIS IS REALLY GOOD.
YOU WANTED TO DO THIS AS, LIKE, A SYMBOLIC THING?
NO...
NOT... ENTIRELY...

IT IS...
WELL, OKAY.
UH...
RIGHT. HERE GOES...
...NMUF...
S'GREAT...
S'LIKE A SORT OF PERFUME TASTE... LIKE CARDAMOM...
WHAT DO YOU MEAN?
IS THERE SOMETHING ELSE I SHOULD HAVE...
UH...
ALEC...?
ALEC... EVERYTHING LOOKS SORT OF...
...STRANGE...
HOW... DO YOU MEAN... "STRANGE"...?
ALEC?
ALEC... I...
OH.
OHHH...

OH, LOOK AT THE SWAMP...
IT'S ALL OF FIRE... MILLIONS OF BIRTHDAY CANDLES...
AND... LOOK AT *ME!* ALL THESE STRANDS OF PEARLY STUFF...
ALEC... WHAT'S *HAPPENED* TO EVERYTHING?
YOU ATE... THE *FRUIT*... ABBY...
YOU ABSORBED... A LITTLE... OF MY *CONSCIOUSNESS*...
...MY *PERCEPTIONS*...
YOU MEAN...
YOU MEAN... *THIS*... IS HOW *YOU* SEE THINGS?
NOT... *ALL*... OF THE TIME...
ONLY... WHEN I... *WISH* TO.
DO YOU... *LIKE* IT?

OH, IT'S...
THESE STRANDS... YOU'RE MADE OF THEM, TOO...
EVERYTHING'S MADE OF THEM... SILKY, LUMINOUS COBWEBS...
AND THESE LITTLE STARS... THESE LITTLE JEWELS OF LIGHT THAT DRIFT ABOUT INSIDE YOU...
I DON'T HAVE ANY OF THOSE...
NO. THOSE... ARE INSECTS...
EVERYTHING'S ALIVE AND...
...AND IT'S ALL MADE FROM THE SAME STUFF!
I NEVER REALIZED...
I NEVER REALIZED...
...THAT THE WORLD...
...WAS LIKE THIS...

SPRING CAME, AND EVERYTHING IN THE WORLD WOKE UP...
MY HAND SHATTERS THE POOL, A HUNDRED GLASS BEADS EXPLODING OUT BETWEEN MY FINGERS.
A BRIEF ANTI-GRAVITY NECKLACE SETTLES AGAINST MY THROAT, COLLAPSING, DISSOLVING, WARM AS IT TRICKLES AWAY...
BELOW THE WATER THE SUDDEN COLD FROTTAGE OF FISH SKIN, SLICK AND SILVER AGAINST MY INSTEP...
IT TWISTS, FLICKERS, DISAPPEARS. THE BUBBLES RISE...
THE THREADLIGHTS, A BLAZING CAT'S CRADLE INSIDE ME, INSIDE HIM...
WHERE WE TOUCH, THE FIBERS MERGE AND INTERTANGLE.
I AM NO LONGER CERTAIN WHERE I END... WHERE HE BEGINS...
I FEEL MY OWN HAND AS HE FEELS IT, A WARM BIRD CAGED WITHIN MY STRONG GREEN FINGERS, PULSE HAMMERING IN ITS BREAST...

A SMEAR OF PLATINUM SCALES BREAKS THE SURFACE, ROLLING, RESUBMERGING. THERE IS A DELICIOUS AMBIGUITY...
LOOKING UP THROUGH HIS EYES: THE PALE WOMAN GAZES DOWN, A BURNING FLOWER ADRIFT ON THE MILK WATER-FALL OF HER HAIR.
ITS LANK TIRS DRAIN CLEAR SABLE BRUSH-STROKES BETWEEN THE LICHENS ENGRAVING MY CHEST...
SHE IS...
...SO BEAUTIFUL...
I...
...AM...
...SO...
...BEAUTIFUL...
WE BLUR TOGETHER, UNRESISTING... THE BUBBLES RISE.
A TIDE OF EMERALDS ENGULFS ME.
I'M FALLING INTO HIM.
I DON'T CARE.

IN HIM, I RIDE THE AMBER SAP, OOZING THROUGH MINIATURE LABYRINTHS. CLUSTERS OF INSECT EGGS BURN LIKE NEBULAE, SUSPENDED IN THEIR UNIQUE AND VINE-WROUGHT COSMOS...
THROUGH HIM, I SPRAWL WITH THE SWAMP, SOPPING, STEAMING, DRAGONFLIES STITCHING NEON THREADS THROUGH THE DAMP AIR SURROUNDING ME...
BEYOND HIM I WRESTLE THE PLANET, SUNK IN LOAM TO MY ELBOWS AS IT ARCHES BENEATH ME, TUMBLING ENDLESSLY THROUGH ENDLESS INK.
THE BARK ENCRUSTS MY FLANKS. THE MOSS CLIMBS MY SPINE TO EMBRACE MY SHOULDERS...
WE... ARE... ONE CREATURE...
...AND ALL...
...THAT THERE IS...
...IS IN US...

TOGETHER WE KNOW THE LIGHT, EXPLODING UPWARD IN A BIRDCLOUD, FRAGMENTING INTO WHIRRING FEATHERED SHRAPNEL, DANCERS IN THE GLARE...
... BUT THE LIGHT IS NOT ALL THAT WE KNOW.
TOGETHER WE BATHE IN RAW LIFE: HONEY ROLLS ACROSS OUR TONGUE. THE FRAGRANCE OF DECAY, MESMERIC AND OVERWHELMING, EXCITES OUR NOSTRILS. WE SAVOR BOTH EQUALLY...
...FOR LIFE IS NOT ALL THAT WE COMPREHEND.
WE ARE THE WORLD.
AMID COILING, LIGHTLESS MAZES DEEP WITHIN US, RODENTS MAKE LOVE AND WAGE VENDETTAS, WITH NEEDLE TEETH THAT TEAR AND SMALL HEARTS THAT SPILL POPPIES ON BLACK EARTH SCENTED WITH URINE.
TENDERNESS. PASSION. VIOLENCE...
MY ENEMY'S BLOOD ERUPTS TO FILL MY MOUTH WITH MOLTEN COPPER.
I CIRCLE WITH THE HAWKMOTHS AT THEIR CONJUGATION, BREATHLESS AT THE ALIEN DESIRES ABSTRACTED IN THEIR DANCE...
THERE IS NO CONTRADICTION...
...ONLY THE PULSE.
THE PULSE WITHIN THE WORLD.
WITHIN US.
WITHIN ME.

IT THROBS. IT BREATHES. IN THE WORLD, IN ITS FIBERS...
THE PULSE QUICKENS, STRANDS TIGHTEN, DRAW TAUT, A CLENCHED GLOVE IN MY STOMACH...
UNDERGROUND, BURIED CLAWS WOUND THE SOIL...
SAVAGE FURROWS FILL WITH MOISTURE...
A FISH TWISTS...
THE BUBBLES RISE...
THE WORLD PULSES...
...AND SHUDDERS...
WITH LIFE...
...AND DEATH...
WITH TIDE...
...AND MAGMA...

....
WITH HIM.
WITH ME.

DOES THIS... UH...
DOES THIS MEAN WE'RE GOING OUT?

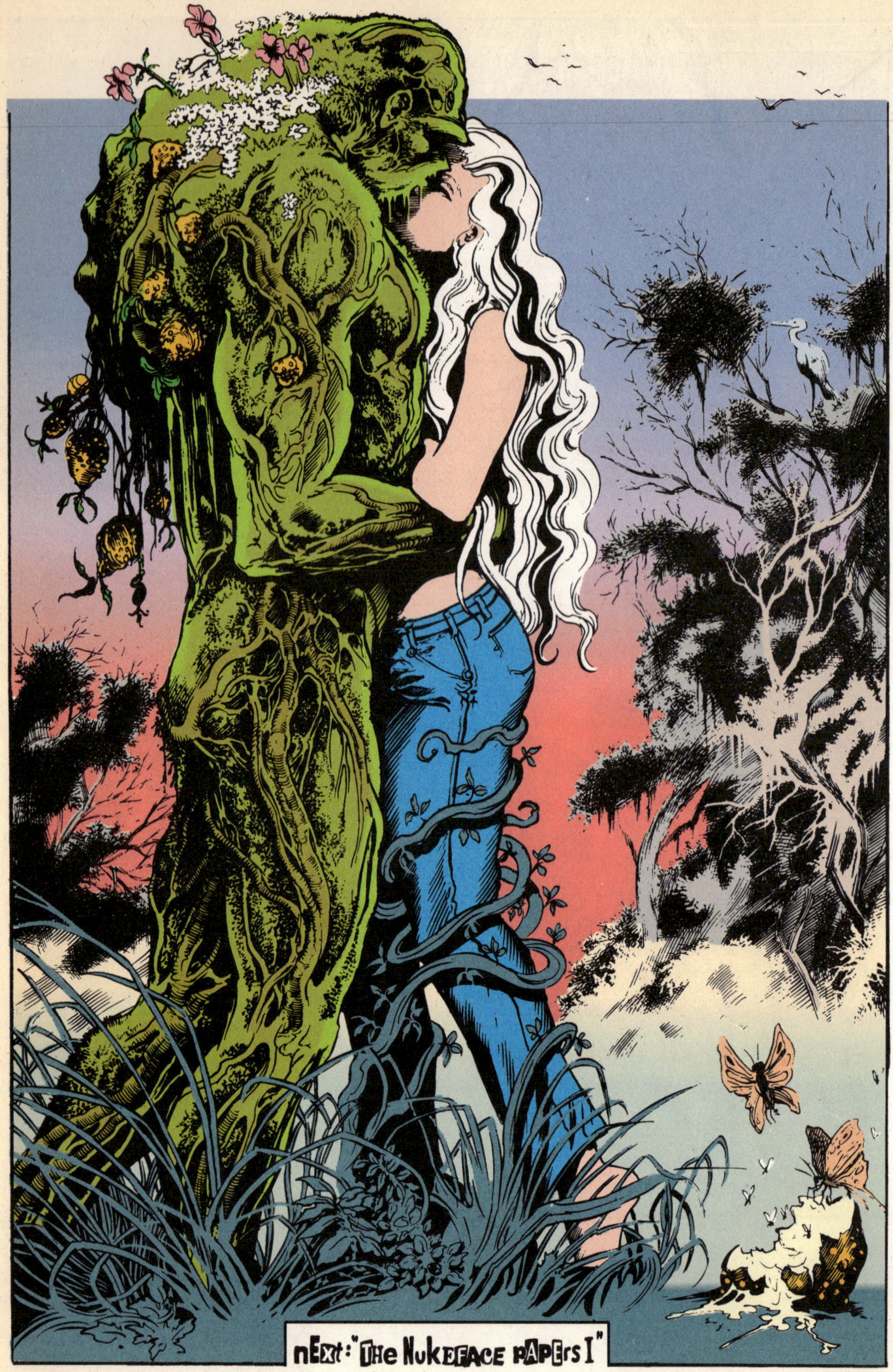
NEXT: "THE NUKEFACE PAPERS I"

RICK VEITCH worked in the underground comics scene before attending the Joe Kubert School of Cartoon and Graphic Art. After graduating, he worked with Stephen Bissette on *Bizarre Adventures* before creating and illustrating *The One*, the innovative Epic Comics miniseries. In addition to writing and drawing an acclaimed run on *Swamp Thing*, he is the creator/cartoonist of *Brat Pack*, *Maximortal* and the dream-based *Rare Bit Fiends*, and a contributing artist on *1963*. He is also the writer and artist of the miniseries *Greyshirt: Indigo Sunset* from America's Best Comics, and the creator of the critically acclaimed graphic novel *Can't Get No* and the spectacularly satirical series *Army@Love* from Vertigo.

ALFREDO ALCALA's graceful, moody inks helped maintain the style on *Swamp Thing* through many penciller changes. DC first employed Alcala's talents in its horror and war comics such as *Ghosts*, *Unexpected*, and *Weird War Tales*. Later he moved on to titles including *All-Star Squadron*, *Savage Sword of Conan*, *Batman*, *Swamp Thing* and countless others for both DC and Marvel. After a long battle with cancer, Alcala passed away in April, 2000.

RON RANDALL has been working professionally as an illustrator and storyteller for over twenty years. He has worked for all the major American comic publishers, including DC, Marvel, Dark Horse and Image, as well as commercial clients such as Disney, Nike, SeaWorld and Sony.

Veteran comics writer and editor **LEN WEIN** is the creator of such memorable characters as Wolverine, the New X-Men and the Human Target, as well as the co-creator (with Bernie Wrightson) of the Swamp Thing. In his long and prolific career he has written for hundreds of titles, encompassing nearly every significant character in the medium. He has also built a successful career in TV animation, scripting such hit series as *X-Men*, *Spider-Man* and *Batman: The Animated Series*.

BERNIE WRIGHTSON, co-creator of the Swamp Thing, has disturbed impressionable readers for more than three decades with his uncanny renderings of imaginary horrors. His recent work in the comics field includes DC's *Batman: The Cult* and Marvel's *The Punisher*.

TATJANA WOOD switched careers from dressmaking to comics coloring in the late 1960s and quickly established herself as one of the top colorists in the field, winning two Shazam awards in the early 1970s.

Over his long and prolific career, **JOHN COSTANZA** has lettered a huge number of comics and has won numerous awards along the way. A cartoonist in his own right, Costanza has also contributed stories and art to a variety of titles, beginning in the late 1960s and continuing right through to the new millennium.